Curing the Addiction to PROFITS:

A supply-side approach to phasing out tobacco

Cynthia Callard
Dave Thompson
Neil Collishaw

Curing The Addiction To Profits

A SUPPLY-SIDE APPROACH TO PHASING OUT TOBACCO

Cynthia Callard, Dave Thompson
and Neil Collishaw

CANADIAN CENTRE FOR POLICY ALTERNATIVES

Canadian Cataloguing in Publication Data
Curing the addiction to profits:
A supply-side approach to phasing out tobacco

Callard, Cynthia
   Curing the addiction to profits : a supply-side approach to phasing out tobacco / Cynthia Callard, Dave Thompson and Neil Collishaw.

Includes bibliographical references.
ISBN 0-88627-436-2

1. Tobacco industry. 2. Tobacco industry – Government policy.
3. Tobacco habit – Prevention.
4. Smoking – Prevention. I. Thompson, Dave II. Collishaw, Neil
III. Canadian Centre for Policy Alternatives. IV. Title.

HD9130.6.C34 2005   338.4'76797   C2005-902678-2

Printed and bound in Canada
Layout: Tim Scarth   Cover design: Laurie Poon

Canadian Centre for Policy Alternatives
Suite 410, 75 Albert Street
Ottawa, ON K1P 5E7
Tel 613 563-1341 Fax 613 233-1453
http://www.policyalternatives.ca
ccpa@policyalternatives.ca

CCPA
CANADIAN CENTRE
for POLICY ALTERNATIVES
CENTRE CANADIEN
de POLITIQUES ALTERNATIVES

ACKNOWLEDGEMENTS

This research was supported with funding from Health Canada and a research grant from the Canadian Tobacco Control Research Initiative (although the opinions expressed do not necessarily reflect those of these funders). We are very grateful to the funding organizations and the individuals who work within them for their ongoing support of public health.

We are also grateful to our colleagues who contributed to the development of this research at a workshop in November 2004: Ron Borland, Roberta Ferrence, Ed Finn, Linda Gama-Pinto, Atul Kapur, Isra Levy, Michael Perley, Byron Rogers, Tom Stephens, Fred Tabachnik, Francis Thompson, Fernand Turcotte, Kate Walker and Elinor Wilson. Research for earlier stages of the paper was undertaken by a capable summer student, Matthew Butler.

Our thanks also go to the Aurora Institute of Vancouver for their seminal analysis of corporate behaviour and the role of corporations in society and for their support for this project.

TABLE OF CONTENTS

PREFACE

The year was 1987, and the Minister of National Health and Welfare, the Honourable Jake Epp, had recently introduced the draft Tobacco Products Control Act as Bill C-51 in the House of Commons. I was the civil servant responsible for the tobacco legislation file. Very quickly, it became clear that we had a tiger by the tail. The tobacco industry pulled out all the stops to defeat or weaken the government's proposal to ban tobacco advertising.

Members of Parliament were assaulted with blizzards of letters arriving, seemingly from ordinary citizens protesting the new law. There were various texts, fonts, styles and paper stocks. It seemed like a genuine grassroots protest. In reality, it was an early example of fake write-in grassroots campaign organized by a corporation in its own private interest—a "grasstops" campaign. The tobacco industry hired high-profile lobbyists; they created fake coalitions of influential citizens ("Coalition 51"); and they bombarded us with reports they arranged to have sent to us from all over the world, from organizations like the Children's Research Unit, the Smokers' Freedom Society, INFOTAB, the World Federation of Advertising, and Freedom of the Right to Enjoy Smoking Tobacco (FOREST). These and other petitioners they sent our way were all financed by the tobacco industry. Their efforts succeeded to some extent; the initial proposal to ban almost all forms of tobacco advertising was weakened somewhat when it was finally adopted by Parliament in 1988.

In 1987 and 1988, I was kept very busy inside the Health Department reacting to one missive after another from the tobacco industry. What kept me going was the belief that the problem would be solved. The proposed new law would surely bring tobacco consumption to an end.

How wrong I was! I suffered from a common delusion; I was so deep in the FOREST that I could not see it for the trees.

Years later, I was to find myself even deeper in a much bigger forest that I once again could not see for the trees. It was Sunday, March 8, 1998 and I was at home in Ferney-Voltaire, France, just across the border from Geneva, Switzerland where I worked at the World Health Organization (WHO) in charge of the Tobacco or Health Program. The telephone was ringing non-stop. Journalists and colleagues were calling me at home from all over the world, demanding an explanation of the story on page one of that day's London Sunday Telegraph. The story began, "The world's leading health organization [WHO] has withheld from publication a study which shows that not only might there be no link between passive smoking and lung cancer but that it could even have a protective effect."

I did not have a copy of the newspaper; I was only dimly aware that our sister agency in Lyon, the International Agency for Research on Cancer (IARC) in Lyon, France had been conducting a study on passive smoking. I had certainly not seen any results from the study.

I and WHO had been ambushed by the tobacco industry. It was only at the end of the next day that we managed to get a news release out of WHO detailing the misinformation in the Sunday Telegraph. "Passive smoking does cause lung cancer, do not let them fool you," screamed the headline on our news release. But it was too little, too late. In a single day, the tobacco industry's public relations machine had made sure that the story initially published in the Sunday Telegraph was news in every corner of the world. IARC and WHO were staffed with good scientists and skilled international health bureaucrats, but these slow-moving bureaucracies' media relations offices were significantly outgunned by the tobacco industry's global public relations machines. IARC did not even have a media relations officer. Their press officer doubled as IARC's librarian!

Later, Elisa Ong and Stanton Glantz at the University of California researched the circumstances surrounding this event, and discovered that the tobacco industry had been tracking the IARC study since 1993, and spent far more in tracking the study and in planning and executing their masterful disinformation campaign than IARC spent to do the study. Ong and Glantz's careful research was published in the respected medical journal The Lancet in April 2000, but received scarcely any media attention. Two years after the fact, the story was "old news."

Tobacco industry misinformation, fanned by a well-oiled public relations machine, operating everywhere in the world, had trumped careful scientific work by well-meaning health professionals working for IARC, WHO and the University of California. To this day, tobacco industry apologists continue to cite the March 8, 1998 edition of the London Sunday Telegraph as "proof" that passive smoking does not cause lung cancer.

These are just two examples of many similar experiences I have had in nearly a quarter-century of full-time work on tobacco control. Now, finally, I am no longer lost in the trees; I can clearly see the forest.

What the tobacco industry was doing to the Canadian government in 1987 and 1988, and to the World Health Organization in 1998 was exactly what it was programmed to do. Tobacco companies are obliged by laws governing corporations to make money for their shareholders. They can only do this by selling more and more cigarettes. So Big Tobacco will never stop beating up on public health policies and public health agencies. After all, their actions threaten cigarette sales, the only route to shareholder profit for tobacco companies. But the monstrous tragedy of this logic is that the more cigarettes they sell, the more their customers will get sick and die.

As long as we continue to allow tobacco companies to exist as for-profit business enterprises, every attempt we make to curb tobacco industry behaviour in the name of public health improvement control will be met by unceasing tobacco company efforts to defeat, attenuate, mitigate, delay, counter or confuse the new knowledge or new policy measures that tobacco companies think might cut into their sales.

We will never succeed in completely phasing out tobacco consumption until we remove profit-making from the tobacco business.

This book clearly spells out just why this must be done and proposes a variety of workable ways that it could be done.

Public health policy makers can choose to continue the grinding ground war against Big Tobacco, making progress slowly, inch by inch, while, globally, we continue to lose ten people a minute, deaths caused by tobacco.

Or they can choose to bring this grinding trench war to a quicker end by changing the very nature of the corporate machine opposing public health improvement — the Big Tobacco corporate machine that is killing five million people per year around the world.

Ultimately, in the name of human decency, the latter choice is to be preferred. But it can only be made legitimately — democratically and collectively. And that means a lot of people would have to agree that taking the profit out of the tobacco business is the right thing to do. Much thought and discussion and debate will be needed before it happens. We hope that this book will fuel such a debate and lead us closer to the beginning of the end of tobacco consumption.

Neil Collishaw
June 2005

For almost half a century, governments have addressed the devastating health consequences of smoking with measures that encourage individuals to adopt healthier lifestyles. The policies deployed to reduce smoking — high tobacco taxes, bans on cigarette promotions, health warning labels, public education, etc. — try to modify the mindset and actions of smokers or potential smokers, which is why they are considered to be "demand-side" interventions. Even though "supply-side" measures have been found effective for other components of public health (like safe drinking water, hospitals, and controlled access to some drugs), they have not yet been recommended or adopted for tobacco control.

Nonetheless, the problems with the current supply side of the tobacco market are well known. In Canada, as elsewhere, cigarettes are sold by a small number of multinational tobacco corporations whose efforts to undermine public health are well known and well documented. The record of their actions has led many to view tobacco corporations as an immoral, unethical, rogue industry.

This view is mistaken. Tobacco corporations can only be immoral and unethical if they have the capacity to make moral and ethical judgments which, we argue, they do not have. Business corporations are instruments created for the sole purpose of facilitating trade and programmed to make decisions aimed at one exclusive goal: the making of money. They are "legal persons," but they are not human. A more accurate metaphor for this social instrument is a machine, a computer program, or a car. Cars can't feel sorry for the people they hurt, and neither can corporations.

Corporations are required under law to act in the "best interests of the shareholder," which has come to have the unequivocal meaning of maximizing profits. They are rule-driven systems and their behaviour is programmed and predictable. In striving to sell more cigarettes and recruit new smokers, they are doing exactly what they were created to do—sell cigarettes—and what they are required to do: maximize the value of the corporation for its owners by making and selling cigarettes as profitably as possible. The rules of corporate law, combined with the forces of the competitive for-profit marketplace, compel them to try to increase tobacco use. Even if a given tobacco corporation were to remove itself or be removed from the tobacco market, other companies would replace it as long as it was in their shareholders' interest to do so. Those who work for tobacco companies have the capacity to value more than profit-making, but they have neither the authority nor the power to impose this personal view on the corporation's sole focus on profit.

This analysis has clear implications for public health. Tobacco companies will seek to sell more cigarettes and, to do this, they will continue to try to defeat, weaken, bypass, and violate tobacco control measures. Health regulators may develop more sophisticated and stringent tobacco control measures, but the companies will reply every time with more sophisticated and imaginative strategies to blunt their effect.

Governments can overcome this problem by adding a "supply-side" approach to their current "demand-side" strategies. This can be done by transferring responsibility for the supply of cigarettes to a type of enterprise that is not driven to seek profits. There are many forms and hundreds of examples of public-interest enterprises, such as cooperatives, public utilities, Crown corporations, and non-profit agencies, that can serve as models for creating a new public-interest tobacco manufacturer that has a legally-binding mandate to help reduce smoking.

One way to implement such a supply-side strategy would be to acquire existing tobacco corporations, through voluntary or legislated purchase, and then transfer responsibility for manufacturing and supplying tobacco to a public-interest enterprise that is given a legislated mandate to reduce smoking. There are many ways in which such an enterprise could be structured, from which we have identified three models—a public agency, a private agency, and a hybrid licensing commission—for more detailed consideration.

Since society pays the health costs associated with smoking, the cost to Canadians of buying tobacco companies is much lower than the cost of leaving them in place to keep smoking rates high. We estimate that acquiring Canadian tobacco operations and implementing a strategy to phase them out would cost from $0 to $15 billion (one is currently in bankruptcy and they all face major law-suits), and that no more than two years' tobacco tax revenues would be required to finance the purchase. The smokers whose taxes would be assigned to this purchase would be the ones who would benefit the most, as they would finally have a cigarette supplier mandated to meet their desire to quit smoking.

This transfer could be managed without immediate inconvenience to smokers, tobacco growers, tobacco manufacturer employees, retailers, or other market stakeholders, much as private sector transfers in ownership do not necessarily affect these stakeholders. Workers and retailers would not stop manufacturing and selling cigarettes, but their new management would direct them to do so in ways that encourage smokers to quit. Instead of being told to fight or undermine measures that help smokers quit, these workers would be challenged to use their entrepreneurial talents to accelerate and improve on them. The knowledge and expertise that is now used to market cigarettes could be re-directed to de-market smoking and to design and manufacture their cigarettes in ways that reduce their attractiveness or addictiveness. Economic incentives that currently increase tobacco use could be transformed into incentives to decrease tobacco use.

The public health goal of reducing tobacco use is—now and for the foreseeable future—in direct conflict with tobacco corporations' mandate to increase profits. The approaches now used to modify tobacco industry behaviour (shaming, punishment, and imposed codes of conduct) wrongly expect the companies to be capable of behaving against their fiduciary responsibilities. Instead, we should focus on the moral, ethical, and legal responsibilities of those who have granted business corporations control over the tobacco market when healthier options are available.

In the long-term, the solution to the smoking problem rests with the bottom line, prohibiting the tobacco companies from continuing to profit from the sale of a deadly, addictive drug. These profits are inevitably used to promote that same addictive product and to generate more sales. If public health is to be the centerpiece of tobacco control—if our goal is to halt this manmade epidemic—the tobacco industry, as currently configured, needs to be dismantled.[1]

David Kessler
Commissioner of the U.S. Food and
Drug Administration, 1990-1997

ONE

Learn from history or be condemned to repeat it

Giving up smoking: good, bad and awful.

On an early summer day in 1963, Canada's first woman Health Minister, Judy LaMarsh, informed Parliament that one of the most commonly used consumer products was lethal.[2] "There is scientific evidence," she affirmed, "that cigarette smoking is a contributory cause of lung cancer." In addition, she added, chronic bronchitis and coronary heart disease were also likely caused by smoking.

Finally the government had confirmed what the *Reader's Digest* and other media were telling worried smokers: there was, indeed, many a cough in a carton.

The political became the personal for Judy LaMarsh that week, as she tried to end her own three-pack a day habit. It's doubtful that many smokers were encouraged by her example. "I feel better now when I wake up in the morning," she told reporters that week, "but the rest of the day is awful." Nor were her fellow parliamentarians encouraging: "They've been sending me packages of cigarettes or envelopes with a cigarette inside," she said. "When I leave the chamber, they offer me a place to smoke."[3] Her interview was reported under the headline "Giving up smoking: good, bad and awful." The headline could have also served to describe the early efforts of her department—ill-prepared for the challenge and undermined by colleagues.

Ms. LaMarsh's admission that cigarettes caused cancer was dramatic news, but the initiatives she announced were far less groundbreaking. She did not suggest that the tobacco companies should stop making cigarettes, nor even that they should change the way they conducted their business. Instead, she reacted in the familiar Ottawa style—she announced she would host a meeting of concerned parties (the term stakeholder was not yet in vogue). Later that year, provincial health ministries, health professional and voluntary health agencies, the tobacco industry and tobacco farmers came to Ottawa to discuss the "problem" of tobacco.

The outcome of the conference was reported to the Commons in November:

> As a result of a very co-operative day and a half the provincial representatives agreed unanimously on the fact that smoking is harmful, and agreed to undertake co-operatively a program of education and research directed toward young people in the country and their commencing the habit.[4]

She assured the House that her department's public education program "would take the form of a positive program and not a program based on fear." Thus the cornerstone of tobacco programming was laid for a quarter-century—up-beat public education aimed primarily at children.

Over forty years have passed since Judy LaMarsh launched this first national initiative on smoking. By some measures, this initiative and its many successors were quite successful. During LaMarsh's time as Health Minister, more than six in 10 Canadian men smoked, as did four in 10 Canadian women.[5] Today, smoking rates have fallen by more than half—only two in 10 Canadian men and women smoke.[6]

From another perspective, four decades of progress appears less heartening.

The actual number of Canadian smokers has only declined by only 15% since the mid-1960s (5 million[7] compared with 6 million),[8] when public measures to reduce tobacco use first began. The number of cigarettes smoked has fallen by only one-quarter (from 53 billion in 1965 to 39.6 billion in 2004).[9] Nor, sadly, has medical science found the once-hoped-for cures for cancer or other tobacco-caused disease: cigarettes continue to claim more than one in five Canadian lives.[10]

By its own measures, the first government initiatives were a profound failure. In 1965, the government pinned its hopes on being effective at reducing youth smoking. "The fruits of the first generation refusing to conform to the past attitudes of its elders will be one of the most exciting victories in man's ever-broadening advance against disease," gushed a Health Canada strategist.[11]

In fact, the vast majority (over 85%) of those who smoke today started smoking after that strategy was adopted. As Judy LaMarsh and her successors were to learn, telling people about the dangers of smoking, and giving them positive messages about quitting did not stop cigarettes from killing thousands of Canadians.

One of the Canadian lives claimed by tobacco may have been that of Judy LaMarsh. In 1980, at the age of 55, she died of pancreatic cancer (one-third of pancreatic cancers are caused by smoking).

Opposing strategies: government and industry

Since those first steps in the early 1960s, Canadian tobacco control efforts have greatly improved. In the evidence-based world of public health, tobacco control interventions have been repeatedly tested, evaluated, improved and amplified. The early efforts to jolly smokers into quitting and to download the responsibility to protect children onto the school system were eventually acknowledged to be insufficient. Gradually a more "comprehensive" approach to controlling tobacco was developed. The accepted understanding of what today would be called best practice for tobacco control expanded to include dozens of measures, many of which are described later.

Tobacco control has followed an evolutionary path. Governments and health agencies learned from their successes and mistakes. They responded to advances in science, assessed changes in public attitudes and in industry actions, and adapted their actions accordingly. The goal of reducing disease has generally guided this evolution (although it has never been free from competing government objectives, like preserving jobs, helping farmers and political allies and getting re-elected). These health measures continue to evolve.

Those trying to reduce disease are not the only ones following an evolutionary, adaptive path. Tobacco companies also responded to changing circumstances. Like governments and health agencies, they responded to science, assessed changes in public attitudes and in government actions. They adapted their actions accordingly and continue to do so. The purpose of their adaptations was not, however, to help smokers quit or to prevent children from smoking or to reduce the harm caused by their products. Their goal was to maintain and increase their profits.

The evolution of tobacco industry strategies to resist public health measures can be traced through documents that were produced as an unexpected consequence of U.S. and Canadian court cases. Hundreds of industry marketing documents were made available as a result of the court challenges launched by Canadian tobacco operations against federal laws banning and restricting cigarette advertising (in 1988 and again in 1997). A far larger cache of documents was released in 1998 when Minnesota Attorney General, Hubert Humphrey III, refused to settle his claim against Big Tobacco unless they agreed to make public the material that had been produced during the discovery phase of the trial. Subsequent U.S. governments made similar conditions, and today over 60 million pages of formerly secret document are available to any researcher with internet access. Because the firms involved were transnationals operating in Canada (RJ Reynolds and Philip Morris, now Altria) or they were owned by the same transnationals operating in Canada (BAT), thousands of documents pertaining to Canada were also released.

The documents do more than substantiate the allegations that tobacco corporate executives lied when they said they did not believe that cigarettes caused disease, lied when they said that cigarettes were not addictive, and lied when they said they did not market to kids. They explain why this behaviour persists. They provide insight into how and why tobacco companies systematically refused to bring their actions into alignment with public health measures and instead persistently attempted to undermine them.

ITL chief executive Paul Pare before the
Standing Committee on Health (Isabelle Committee), 1969

First; has it been scientifically established that smoking causes the diseases charged against it? The Canadian tobacco industry respectfully submits that this has not been established and welcomes the opportunity to place before this Committee an abundance of evidence to that effect.

ITL Chairman, Jean-Louis Mercier before the
Standing Committee on Health, November 1987

Ms Copps: Mr. Mercier, is it the position of your council that lung cancer can be caused by smoking?

Mr. Mercier: It is not the position of the industry that tobacco causes any disease. Our position is that epidemiological studies are essentially statistical comparisons. All they can demonstrate is an association. They cannot and will not demonstrate a cause and effect relationship.

The first wave: Public education and industry disinformation

The first health initiatives, as discussed, aimed to reduce smoking by informing people of the harms of smoking, encouraging smokers to quit and teaching kids that they shouldn't smoke. Hopes were placed that the next generation (and during the sixties generational differences were much discussed!) would act on the information provided them in schools and would make the "smart" decision not to smoke. These public education efforts continue to this day, and many experts continue to believe that such programs are valuable in motivating smokers to quit and in inoculating children against pressure to smoke.

Tobacco companies responded very differently than governments to the disturbing news that their products were killing its best customers. They did not seek to educate smokers or to discourage children from smoking. Their efforts were focused on the objective of keeping cigarette sales high. With that objective, they set out to undermine the health educational campaigns.

For decades, one Canadian tobacco executive after another denied the harmfulness of cigarettes. At the meeting hosted by Judy LaMarsh in 1963, Imperial Tobacco's Chief Executive Officer, Paul Paré, presented a report that his British boss described as "a brief which sets out very well the scientific evidence to date that contradicts or does not support the anti-smoking charges."[12] At the next parliamentary review six years later, the denial was repeated: "has it been scientifically established that smoking causes the diseases charged against it? The Canadian tobacco industry respectfully submits that this has not been established."[13] Twenty years later, the industry's tune had barely changed when the Imperial Tobacco chief next appeared before Parliament in 1987. "It was not the position of the tobacco industry that tobacco causes any disease."[14]

Were these denials lies? Is it possible that Paul Paré and Jean-Louis Mercier and the other industry heads who testified before Parliament were caught in some mass self-delusion?

The documents show that by the time Paul Paré told Parliament that the evidence disproved the link between smoking and disease his own company scientists had come to the conclusion that the link was proven. Senior officials of the company received numbered copies of the scientists' reports.

The public denials created confusion in the public mind and undermined the health information campaigns run by governments and health agencies, the counseling of physicians and the encouragement of concerned families to help smokers quit. By creating a false sense of controversy about established medical science the companies knew they could keep more smokers from quitting. As long as smokers could tell themselves "it's not really proven," they were less likely to quit.

The deliberativeness of undermining public education is shown in a 1985 strategy document of Imperial Tobacco, which compared its worst case projection of everyone believing that smoking was dangerous with its objective of making sure that no more than 60% of Canadians believe that smoking is "dangerous."[15]

The same disinformation strategies were used in subsequent decades to undermine government campaigns to reduce exposure to second-hand smoke. In the early 1980s, Imperial Tobacco's Montreal laboratory conducted the first known tests on the cancer causing properties of second-hand smoke—and found it was as dangerous as inhaled smoke.[16] After the U.S. Surgeon General reported in 1986 that second-hand smoke was dangerous,[17] the companies similarly created confusion about the science evidence in order to blunt the impact of government education programs. By this time their own credibility problem led them to engage other experts to do the talking on their behalf. They secretly hired academics to sell the message that it was "sick building syndrome" and not cigarette smoke that was the main problem.[18] They also paid the Canadian Hotel Association and Canadian Restaurant and Food Services Association[19] to propose that additional ventilation could be installed to reduce the health risk.

The second wave: Lawmaking and lawbreaking

The shortcomings of a strategy based on education alone quickly became apparent to government and, in the early 1970s, on the recommendation of the Isabelle Committee and the urging of the health community, the Health Ministry began to prepare to support its education efforts with policy measures. At that time, the only constraint on tobacco marketing or manufacture was the never-enforced 1908 law that forbade providing cigarettes to children under 16.

The Health Ministry aimed to impose three controls on tobacco companies: an end to cigarette marketing, warning messages on cigarettes and the production of less toxic cigarettes. Bill C-248, the *Cigarette Products Act*, included measures to ban cigarette advertising, require health warnings on cigarette packages and vending machines and set maximum levels for nicotine and other constituents. When Health Minister John Munro introduced Bill C-248 in June 1971, eight years had elapsed since his predecessor Judy LaMarsh had launched the government's first education efforts.

Bill C-248 died before parliamentarians had a chance to debate its merits. An anonymous history of the time found among the Philip Morris documents relates how the industry lobbyists were able to quickly defeat the bill. "[I]n June 1971, all our worst fears were realized with the introduction to Parliament of Bill C-248, the *Cigarette Products Act*," he wrote. "A high level 'lobbying' activity was initiated and cabinet support was not forthcoming for second reading."[20] Exactly how high level the lobbying was is hinted by another industry official, who reports that John Munro was forced to apologize to the tobacco companies after their "vociferous response" got the ear of Prime Minister Trudeau.

Although the industry won the battle of C-248, they lost important subsequent legislative battles and the measures proposed first proposed to Parliament in 1971 were eventually adopted by Parliament some 17 years later.

It's not accurate to say that for each public health action there was an equal and opposite tobacco industry reaction. But it is accurate to say that the broad general aim of tobacco companies (to make money by selling cigarettes) was diametrically opposed to the public health goal (of reducing disease by ending tobacco use).

Illustrations of the opposing direction of industry and government actions are plentiful.

In the early 1990s, tobacco taxes were significantly increased and cigarette sales fell accordingly. The companies responded by selling their cigarettes to people willing to smuggle them back into Canada at discount prices. In response to this industry-supported smuggling crisis, governments in five provinces lowered taxes in 1994.

In an attempt to control smuggling, the federal government imposed an export tax of $8 per carton in February 1992. The tobacco companies responded by threatening to close production in Canada. The tax was withdrawn six weeks later.

In 1994, the government considered requiring that all cigarettes be sold in plain packages (they were looking for initiatives to reduce the impact of lowering taxes). The tobacco companies threatened a trade challenge under NAFTA.[21] The government made no further moves towards implementing plain packaging.

In 2001, the government proposed to ban the terms "light" and "mild" on cigarette packages. The industry again threatened trade challenges in addition to threatening other legal actions. They also signaled that they would use other package elements like colour-coding to continue to convey to smokers that there was a difference between brand types. The government has not moved forward on the 2001 announcement that such terms would be banned.

In March, 2002, the Saskatchewan Legislature passed a law banning the display of cigarette packages in stores where children were allowed. Manitoba passed a similar law the following year. The industry court challenge succeeded in delaying both laws for many months.

In recent years, several measures have proposed as part of a comprehensive tobacco demand reduction strategy, including: tax increases, bans on smoking in public places, plain packaging, modified cigarette designs (to reduce cigarette- caused fires), ending the deception caused by so-called light cigarettes, graphic health warning messages, removing cigarettes from view in retail outlets, etc. Some of these measures have been put in place. None of them has come into place without tobacco companies trying to defeat the measures before they were introduced, trying to pervert their impact after they were introduced, or sabotaging their implementation in ways that dulled their impact.

The third wave: The fight for public opinion

Frustrated by the relentless intransigence of tobacco corporations and their frequent political successes, governments launched campaigns for the hearts and minds of the public. By turning the spotlight on the actions of "Big Tobacco," some governments and health activists hoped to accelerate the adoption of health policies. In Canada this strategy is usually referred to as "denormalization," and it was adopted by Canada's multi-sectoral tobacco control agency in the late 1990s as an additional goal to the 1960s and 1970s goals of helping smokers quit (cessation) and stopping non-smokers from becoming addicted (prevention), and the 1980s addition of protection of non-smokers from second-hand smoke.

Governments were decades behind the tobacco industry in the fight for public opinion. Long before denormalization campaigns were launched, the industry worked to normalize smoking. They sought to "influence, modify or change public opinion to the industry, smokers and smoking, to create a more favourable climate however directly or indirectly."[22] To do this, they collaborated (a less charitable analysis would be to say they conspired) at a global level in order to ensure that all tobacco companies in all countries delivered essentially the same messages to all governments and all media. These messages changed over time, but the strategic objective did not: each of them was aimed at maintaining the ability of the companies to sell cigarettes with as few constraints as possible.

The global collaboration/conspiracy began in 1977, when the most senior officials of the world's largest tobacco companies (Philip Morris, Imperial Tobacco, BAT, RJ Reynolds, Reemstma, Rothmans International, and Gallaher) gathered at Shockerwick House, a Georgian era mansion near Bath, England.[23] They agreed that despite their competition in the market place, they needed to work together to convince the global public of three things:

- that smoking was socially acceptable;
- that there were benefits of smoking;
- that there were other things that could cause lung cancer.

In short order, the companies created an agency to coordinate their efforts, the International Committee on Smoking Issues (ICOSI). Tellingly, the only companies which could be members of ICOSI were those which were purely for-profit free-enterprise companies (state monopolies were not to be invited to join).*

In didn't take long after the meeting in Shockerwick House for the companies to begin work in earnest. A Social Acceptability Working Party with membership from all the companies was tasked with coming up with recommendations for "counter-measures" to public health initiatives. The companies had a clear view of the challenge before them:

> It is important to note that not all industries need countermeasures. Many businesses simply have to concern themselves with traditional business functions of product development, production, quality control, marketing, etc.

* In 1977, even in the so-called free world, many tobacco companies were owned and operated by governments (including tobacco monopolies in France, Italy, Austria and Japan).

However, around the world, there are individual governments and other public groups who have put great pressure on the tobacco industry. The industry (and in some instances, companies within the industry) must undertake steps to nullify or weaken the thrusts that are being made against the industry on social acceptability issues. These thrusts against the industry in the area of public smoking include attempts to:

- *restrict or ban smoking;*
- *intimidate smokers into not smoking because of social pressure;*
- *arouse general public sentiment against smoking;*
- *limit the ability of the industry to competitively market their products.*

To meet this challenge, the committee of tobacco transnationals unabashedly recommended five forms of counter-measures be used to keep people smoking: [24]

- **Legislative countermeasures**
  Corporations should "block, nullify, modify or delay pending legislation" and "have existing legislation, particularly tax legislation, repealed or amended in favor of the industry."

- **Regulatory countermeasures**
  Corporations are urged to meet with officials to "encourage legislative oversight."

- **Coalition countermeasures**
  Corporations are urged to organize their allies and "educate, mobilize and motivate smokers and the "tobacco family" to stand up and speak out for the industry on public issues."

- **Electoral countermeasures**
  Tobacco corporations are urged to electioneer for favourable governments: "the objective of this type of countermeasure is the very clear

cut one of winning on a specific election day. The target is the voting public."

- **Public climate countermeasures**
  Corporations are encouraged to turn public opinion in their favour and to frame tobacco in ways that continue smoking. "Convince the general public that: other people's smoking is not hazardous to their health; smoking is a matter of choice; smoking problems are best handled by voluntary private action, not public decrees; smokers are constructive members of society; it is the zealotry of anti-smokers that is at the root of any social problems of smoking."

Twenty-five years later, these five countermeasures continue to be employed to delay public health efforts to reduce smoking:

- Tobacco corporations use **legislative countermeasures** to oppose virtually every proposed tobacco law, and often succeed in defeating and delaying them. (The decision of the governments of Saskatchewan and Manitoba to ban the retail display of cigarettes was delayed by over a year as a result of a tobacco court challenge,[25] and the proposals for plain packaging of Canadian cigarettes has languished so long that it can only be considered to have been successfully defeated.)[26]

- They have used **regulatory countermeasures** to weaken the application of tobacco laws and sponsorship advertising and bar events to avoid bans on lifestyle advertising.

- They have used **coalition countermeasures** to mobilize communities to speak on their behalf. They have created groups like the "Alliance for Sponsorship Freedom" to fight advertising restrictions, and retailers to fight restrictions on in-store promotions.[27]

- The corporations have used **electoral countermeasures** by supporting governments friendly to their interest. They donated to free-enterprise political parties and often loaned their staff to support in election efforts of these parties.[28]

- Their **public climate countermeasures**, like the tobacco industry subsidized smokers' web-site mychoice.ca./monchoix.ca,[29] aim to reinforce the view that smoking is an adult "choice," and that smoking issues are best managed by private voluntary action.

The current wave: New strategies, same goal

The release of tobacco industry documents has forced tobacco corporations to change their public position on many issues, but it has not stopped them from trying to influence public opinion in ways that encourage smoking.

After the Minnesota settlement resulted in the release of documents detailing the activities of the industry (including many Canadian documents), the companies found they had to adapt their public relations strategies. With millions of pages of documentation made public, they could no longer maintain that they did not believe nicotine to be addictive, or that they did not believe cigarette smoke or second-hand smoke to be dangerous, or that they did not market to kids. They responded by re-framing the public debate, and moving public discussion into new topic areas: how important it is for kids not to smoke, and how they care about the community.

Because of the spill-over of American media across the border, many Canadians are familiar with Philip Morris' heavily advertised attempts to revamp its image. It changed its baggage-laden name to the loftier-sounding Altria. The old messages denying addiction and disease were removed from the web-sites and a new message appeared: "Philip Morris USA agrees with the overwhelming medical and scientific consensus" about the diseases caused by smoking, nicotine addiction and the equal harmfulness of low-tar cigarettes.[30] Philanthropic activities were promoted and, more controversially, so was telling kids not to smoke. "Think. Don't smoke," they told children and "Talk. They'll listen," they told parents.

The new campaigns deflected attention away from the role tobacco companies play in youth smoking, and their responsibility to prevent it. They also shifted the focus to friends as the reason for youth smoking and to parents as those responsible for preventing it. The campaigns also put the Philip Morris name back on television, and in the hands of the millions of American school children who received Philip Morris anti-smoking book-covers at school.[31] Clever marketing indeed: independent researchers found that the messages were counterproductive at reducing youth smoking, and that the Philip Morris ads made kids more open to smoking.[32]

British American Tobacco (BAT, which makes most of the cigarettes sold in Canada) has also launched public campaigns that downplay the health risks associated with their products and focus on improving the reputation of the company in a broader context. BAT companies have focused on corporate social responsibility and their "socio-economic contribution."

The companies are more open about their campaigns against public health initiatives. The Canadian Tobacco Manufacturers Council (representing the three multinational companies) runs three campaigns which combine the countermeasures identified thirty years earlier. These campaigns create third-party coalitions:

- to try to defeat public health bans on smoking in public places and workplaces and replace them with ventilation standards (the "Fair Air" campaign "supports the hospitality industry in their efforts to respond to financially crippling and unilateral smoking bans");

- to mobilize retailers to defeat bans on tobacco promotions at retail, and to replace them with industry-run education campaigns to discourage sales to youth (Operation ID "aims to eliminate underage tobacco access");

- to change the public climate through a smoker's rights group (My-choice.ca — "a platform which provides adult smokers with the information and tools to participate in the public policy discussion on tobacco control").[33]

Examples of promotions for Export A cigarettes, 1986 — 2005

TOP RIGHT

1986 (pre Tobacco Products Control Act)
No legal restrictions. Tobacco companies voluntarily place health warnings, human figures are used.

Shark. Skin.

Greg Norman, "The Shark," takes on Fred Couples, Nick Faldo and Nick Price at the 1998 Export 'A' Inc. Skins Game at the National Golf Club of Canada, July 29th & 30th on CBC.

LEFT

1990-95 (Tobacco Products Control Act)
Promotion of corporate sponsored events allowed. Human figures used, but health warnings aren't.

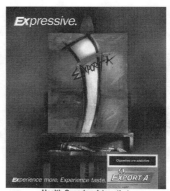

Health Canada advises that
smoking is addictive and causes lung cancer,
emphysema and heart disease.

BOTTOM RIGHT

1996 (post Tobacco Products Control Act, but before Tobacco Act)
Industry voluntarily refrains from using human figures, and includes health warnings.

Examples of promotions for Export A cigarettes, 1986—2005

TOP LEFT

April 1997—October 2000
Tobacco Act allows sponsorship promotions in public venues (like billboards). Human figures are present, but health warnings aren't.

RIGHT

October 2000—October 2003
Tobacco Act allows sponsorship promotions, but only on-site, in publication and in bars. Some companies continue to run retail promotions, and they all start promotional events in bars. Cigarette girls return to Canada.

BOTTOM LEFT

After October 2003—
Sponsorship Ends (in theory), but sponsored promotions continue. Some companies continue to run retail promotions, bar promotions and web-sites.

A closer look

*The ingenuity of tobacco marketing
departments undermines advertising bans*

Tobacco marketing provides a striking example of how tobacco compa-nies have been able to undermine public health goals. Instead of com-plying with marketing restrictions (either voluntary codes or laws), they found ways of getting around the restrictions. Despite the passage of laws and the creation of a global treaty calling for a total ban on tobacco advertising, the companies have never shown any willingness to stop marketing their products. Instead, they have shown great ingenuity in creating and exploiting loopholes in any law or advertising code.

The lack of good faith in the development of voluntary codes was clearly expressed by industry officials who explained that the reason the companies agreed in 1971 to adopt a stronger voluntary advertising code was to forestall future legislation. "Our strategy as an industry then became one of making some concessions, to lose the battle in order to win the war, or in other words to throw the government a bone," wrote an Imperial Tobacco historian of the decision to strengthen the adver-tising code.[34] Among their self-imposed constraints was an agreement not to advertise on television, to place health warning messages on ad-vertisements and on packages, and to stop using promotional coupons. The code was not a real impediment to the companies: "The restrictions to date have still left [the marketing department] a substantial area of activity...The ingenuity of the marketing people is to be commended."[35] The voluntary advertising code was not intended to reduce tobacco mar-keting, it was intended to get rid of an unwanted law.

The ineffectiveness of the voluntary code at reducing smoking en-couraged the development of a legislative ban on tobacco advertising Bill C-51, which later became the *Tobacco Products Control Act* (TCPA) which was proclaimed in 1988. Like the 1971 legislative proposals, this law would eventually be defeated by the tobacco companies. Their court challenge helped establish that the freedom of expression guarantees in the then-new *Charter of Rights and Freedoms* also applied to commercial speech. A divided Supreme Court struck down the TPCA in 1995 saying that the government would need to provide more evidence that a total ban on advertising was necessary before they would agree to such total restrictions. Like the voluntary code before it, the statutory ban on advertising did not deter tobacco companies from energetically marketing cigarettes. Once again, the ingenuity of the marketers was called on to ensure a substantial area of marketing activity.

The TPCA said that advertising was banned, and that sponsorship promotions could not be under cigarette brand names; only corporate names could be used. This exception had been included under pressure from arts groups who wanted to be able to recruit non-branded sponsors (like "Imasco"). The companies did not remove branding from their sponsorships, they just created branded companies. New wholly-owned companies—like Players Racing Ltd., Du Maurier Arts Ltd., Matinee Fashion Ltd., Export A Inc.—were created to flout the law. Within a very short period, lifestyle **direct** advertising had been replaced with lifestyle **sponsorship** advertising.

After the defeat of the *Tobacco Products Control Act* in September 1995, the tobacco companies developed a new voluntary code, which they announced immediately after the then Health Minister, Diane Marleau, announced that a new law banning tobacco advertising would be in place, and that her department would produce the evidence justifying a total ban as the Supreme Court had requested. The new law restricting tobacco advertising (Bill C-71, the *Tobacco Act*) was introduced a year later, and fell far short of a complete ban. C-71 was rushed through Parliament. (This was the first tobacco law to have closure applied, indicating the absence of broad political support), and was proclaimed at the end of April 1997. The government backed even further away from a complete ban when the Prime Minister's office announced that restrictions on sponsorship advertising would be postponed for three years, and that sponsorship would not be banned for six years).

Decades later, the tobacco companies are still able to apply their ingenuity to finding ways of overcoming voluntary or legislated controls on tobacco marketing. Traditional advertisements have been replaced by more covert marketing practices. Tobacco brands continue to be promoted in Canada on race cars, by cigarette girls, in retail displays, on webs-sites, in imported magazines, in direct mail, in web-sites and on

the movie screen. The promotion budgets of the Canadian companies
are large—they spend over $170 million a year on promotional market-
ing, including more than $70 million on payments to retailers to ensure
that cigarettes are the most prominently marketed good in the stores
frequented by children.

"Light cigarettes—a third alternative to quitting."

Just as the companies worked to overcome the attempts by the public to
ban cigarette advertising, they also found ways to turn the goal of making cigarettes less harmful into a marketing opportunity to reduce fears
about smoking.

During the 1970s, the government requested tobacco companies to
lower the average tar levels of their cigarettes by increasing the proportion of their sales of lower-tar cigarettes. The firm belief among health
researchers at that time was that if cigarette smoke contained less tar
then smokers would inhale less tar and then they would suffer less se-
vere health effects.

The tobacco scientists were also working to find a way to make cigarettes less harmful. But they were even more eager to find a way to make
cigarettes **seem** less harmful.[36] Their efforts to create "safer" cigarettes
that they were willing to market floundered. They could not find a way

to make a conventional cigarette safer, and they weren't willing to take conventional cigarettes off the market and replace them with non-burning cigarettes or other alternative nicotine delivery systems.

They were, however, enormously successful at finding a way to make cigarettes seem less harmful. The marketing of "light" cigarettes allowed many smokers to be fooled into believing that by changing the cigarette they smoked they were doing something for their health and that this was an excuse not to quit just yet. This new generation of deceptively designed, deceptively labeled and deceptively marketed products gave the companies a whole new lease on life.

The first step the tobacco companies used to find a less harmful cigarette was to establish a way of measuring harmfulness. One approach they used was to develop toxicity tests for cigarette smoke. One toxicity test involved painting the tar of cigarettes on the skin of mice to see how quickly tumors formed.[37] Another exposed bacteria to cigarette smoke to see how quickly mutations would appear.[38] A third involved the creation of an index to measure the relative toxicity of the smoke from one cigarette compared with another.[39] The companies never publicized the results of these tests and they never applied the lessons from these tests to their cigarette designs.

Instead, the tobacco companies adopted as a measurement of harmfulness the amount of tar that was left behind when a cigarette was smoked by a machine. They raced to produce cigarettes which gave lower levels on these machine tests, and found ways of poking holes in the paper or using less tobacco, or changing the filter to lower the machine level.

When the companies found that smokers didn't like these new lower-tar cigarettes (smokers said it was like "sucking on air"), they set out to find a way of making a cigarette that gave a low machine reading (i.e. that could be marketed as safer), but which gave the smoker as much nicotine-laden tar as the smoker wanted. Instead of finding cigarettes that were actually safer, they tried to make cigarettes that allowed smokers to "cheat" and get more smoke than the machine did (they called these cigarettes "compensatible" as they allowed smokers to "compensate" for the lower machine readings by smoking differently than the machine).

To develop these cigarettes the companies knew they needed a machine that smoked like a real smoker, so they developed one — in secret. They used their new "puff duplicator" extensively to study smokers and to test cigarettes — but never informed the people who bought their cigarettes that the numbers on the side of the package were no indication of how much smoke they would actually inhale.

One reason that the companies kept quiet about the shortcomings of light cigarettes was that they quickly learned that these cigarettes were very helpful at forestalling people who wanted to quit smoking from actually doing it. "Pre-lights, these concerned consumers had a limited range of options open to them — essentially quit or cut down. Fortunately for the tobacco industry, neither of these two approaches proved very successful for smokers," wrote Imperial Tobacco marketer Bob Bexon in 1984.[40] Light cigarettes gave worried smokers the feeling that they were doing something for their health, even thought hey could not quit. "It is useful to consider lights more as a third alternative to quitting and cutting down," he concluded. Bexon would later become CEO to Imperial Tobacco, and their Players "Light" cigarette would become Canada's best selling brand.

Government studies showing that so-called low tar and "light" cigarettes were not safer than regular cigarettes would not become public for twenty years after the industry knew this to be the case. To this day, many smokers continue to believe that cigarettes sold in packages marked "light" are less harmful or less addictive than cigarettes sold without that label.[41]

Industry youth access campaigns undermined
public education campaigns

As pressure built for more effective ways to prevent further generations from becoming addicted to tobacco, governments looked to measures to stop the marketing of cigarettes — including bans on advertising and measures to prohibit the sale to those who were underage. The industry resisted and adapted to advertising bans, as we saw above. They also responded to the youth access issue by adapting it to their purpose.

Beginning in the early 1980s, in Canada and elsewhere, the companies launched programs purportedly aimed at preventing youth access to cigarettes. The internal reports from the period show that these programs were not intended to actually reduce youth smoking, but were intended to improve their public image and to build relationships with legislators, regulators and other community leaders.[42] By appearing to agree with the goal of reducing youth smoking, the industry hoped to delay measures that would actually achieve it.

The industry campaigns delivered messages that reinforced the companies' cigarette advertisements. These campaigns reminded youth that smoking is "for adults," which the industry knew to be one of the most effective marketing messages to their youngest market. The industry's own research had shown that children started smoking because they used it as a rite of passage into adulthood and an expression of their rebellious individuality.[43] The youth smoking campaigns also stressed "the law" as the reason that kids shouldn't smoke. This strengthened the use of cigarettes as a way of rebelling against authority. (Telling teenagers not to do something will increase the desire of many of them to do it!) The focus on lawfulness also weakened the efforts of governments, doctors and the media to focus on the health consequences of smoking.

Back to the future

It would be reassuring to think that the measures steadily implemented over 40 years to reduce smoking reflect the gradual advance of public health science, an improvement in decision making and the adoption of evidence-based measures in disease control. It is less reassuring to know that many of the measures that we are still unable to see implemented were first proposed in our great-grandfather's time.

In 1903, cigarette smoking in Canada was not widespread (only 29 cigarettes per person were smoked each year).[44] Nonetheless, a majority of Members of Parliament—on a free vote—voted to prohibit tobacco,[45] and a bill to that effect was introduced the following year. Prime

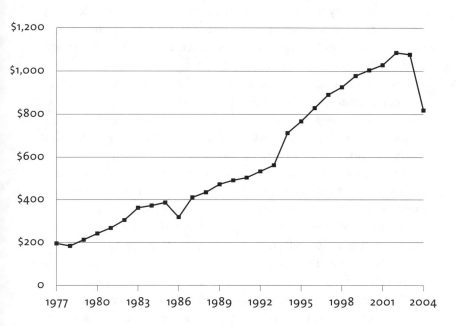

Imperial Tobacco Canada Ltd earnings
(before taxes and extraordinary expenses) from tobacco sales
1977–2004, adjusted for inflation (millions of $2004)

Minister Wilfrid Laurier took the minority view against prohibition, and it was clearly a powerful minority. The law was not brought to a final vote before the parliamentary session ended.[46] This House of Commons resolution came five years before Canada banned opium (in 1908) and twenty years before it extended the ban to heroin, cocaine and marijuana (in 1923).[47]

In 1914, Parliament struck a "Special Committee on Cigarette Evils" to hear proposals on how to respond to concerns about smoking. (Even after the strategy of denormalization has been adopted, it is hard to imagine a parliamentary committee using such a title today!) During that review, the legendary children's advocate and founder of the Children's Aid Society, J.J. Kelso, recommended that tobacco advertising should be restricted, that cigarettes not be sold in all retail outlets but restricted to specialty stores, that movies not portray women smoking and that cigarette taxes be raised to discourage smoking.[48]

Nearly a century later, J.J. Kelso must be turning in his grave. Tobacco advertising is only restricted, not banned and is only a mouse-click away. Young people still watch movie stars smoke on screen, they can buy cigarettes in any one of 60,000 retail outlets and they can buy a pack of cigarettes with their lunch money.

The proudest achievement of a century of science is that we can now count tobacco's dead and dying much more accurately in than in J.J. Kelso's day, or when the House of Commons was first looking for ways to get rid of tobacco. In the past century, we have learned how to count tobacco deaths, but we have not yet learned how to prevent them.

Although smoking rates have fallen, tobacco companies have continued to make and sell cigarettes in large numbers. Even when the number of cigarettes sold in Canada has dropped, industry profits have increased. In 1965, Imperial Tobacco Canada reported net earnings of $13.3 million,[49] the equivalent of $82 million in 2004. By 2002 these profits had grown to $1 billion. During the past 25 years, Imperial Tobacco has only failed to increase its year-over-year profits in real terms on three occasions.[50]

Canadian governments have sought to change the way in which cigarettes are marketed (and, to a lesser extent, made), but they have done little to change the fact that they *are* made, or the motivations behind those who make them. When governments, including Canadian governments, have used coercive measures—in the form of statute law, of litigation and the threat of both—it has been to change the behaviour of tobacco companies, not to change the structure, mindset or operating principles of these companies. We have been flailing at alligators with wooden paddles, instead of draining the swamp.

Tobacco control successes over four decades suggest that the current comprehensive measures are effective, and that they are necessary to reduce smoking. But our slow progress in reducing absolute levels of smoking suggests that these measures are not sufficient to end tobacco use, or even to reduce it to minimal levels.

Missing from the comprehensive strategy that Canadian (and other) governments have adopted is a plan to change the way cigarettes are supplied. New "supply-side" measures to expand our current strategies are now proposed: Australian health researcher Ron Borland has suggested that tobacco marketing should be controlled by a public agency with a legislated mandate to provide cigarettes in ways that reduce harm.[51] Other proposed strategies include banning tobacco and penalizing possession of tobacco by young persons (such measures are on the books in Alberta and Nova Scotia, but have not been actively enforced).

We suggest that rather than increasing the regulations on tobacco marketing or developing criminal-law penalties on those who use cigarettes, we can be more effective by transforming big tobacco into a public health ally.

The question is—can a tobacco company change?

TWO

A source of the problem: the business corporation

Rogue industry or blood-sucking parasite?

With a forty-year history of killing their customers and undermining attempts to keep them alive, it is not surprising that tobacco corporations are the least admired members of Canada's business community. Even their own pollsters tell them they are at the bottom of the reputation heap.[52] They're not only worse than other businesses, says Canada's leading anti-smoking group, they're in a league of their own: "The tobacco industry is a rogue industry that operates outside the norms of legitimate, ethical business."[53]

Calling the tobacco sector a "rogue industry" suggests that there is something unique and aberrant about tobacco corporations that results in their acting in ways that other corporations would not.

Some people describe the role tobacco corporations play in the spread of smoking to the role of mosquitoes in the spread of malaria. Just as the mosquito is the vector of malaria, tobacco corporations are characterized as the "vector for tobacco-attributable morbidity and mortality."[54] This is more than a clever metaphoric device to compare tobacco corporations with insects; it also helps transfer knowledge from infectious disease control to the newer challenges of cancer, heart and lung disease.

The malaria parasite that is transmitted by mosquitoes kills two million people each year, which is less than half as many as are killed by tobacco products. A complete malaria program includes treatment for those who are infected and prophylactic drugs to prevent the onset of disease among those who have been bitten. It also includes protective bed nets to stop people from being bitten, special prevention drugs for those traveling to malarial zones, and measures to reduce the number of mosquitoes. This is not unlike the comprehensive set of measures used to treat and prevent tobacco-caused disease.

The anopheles mosquitoes and the tobacco industry both cause millions of deaths. But those trying to control malaria waste no time castigating the mosquito for its blood-thirsty ways, condemning them as "rogue insects," or expecting them not to bite. They know that mosquitoes are not capable of behaving any differently because their genetic programming compels them to draw blood. Mosquitoes have no other choice. Nor do they have qualms about the fact that their survival condemns millions to death. Mosquitoes, after all, are not human.

And this, perhaps, is where the comparison with tobacco corporations is particularly helpful. Because corporations are not human either. Just like mosquitoes, they have no capacity for moral decision-making. Just like mosquitoes, they are programmed to act in predictable ways, even though doing so results in the deaths of millions.

Not inhuman, just not human

A corporation exists in law, but has no other real form. Although corporations share some of the legal rights of persons, and are created, directed and run by humans, it is not appropriate to think of them, metaphorically, as human. If we anthropomorphize corporations, then we give them human qualities (like compassion, remorse, or joy) that they are not capable of having. If we think of them as human, then we will expect them to include moral or emotional considerations into their decisions and actions. They do not have this capacity.

The people who work in or hold shares in a corporation have human qualities, but the corporation itself does not, any more than a ship has the feelings of the feelings of those who built, own or sail upon her. A more accurate metaphor for a corporation is a machine, a computer program, or a car. Cars can't feel sorry for the people they hurt. And neither can business corporations.

The corporation is a legal instrument created for the sole purpose of facilitating trade, and it is programmed to do one thing exclusively — to maximize profits. The corporation has no moral responsibilities, and is incapable of feeling guilty about this selfish tendency. It does, however, have a legal responsibility to act in the best interests of its shareholders.

Tobacco corporations, like all business corporations, are not evil, and they are not good; they are incapable of any moral judgment or culpability. Like other rule-driven systems, their behaviour is programmed and predictable. In striving to sell more cigarettes and recruit new smokers, they are doing exactly what they were created to do and what they are required to do (i.e. make money). The visible hand of corporate law and the invisible hand of the marketplace both compel tobacco corporations to try to increase tobacco use.

In order to understand why tobacco corporations go on killing people and undermining public health policies, we have to understand the structures and characteristics of the business corporation as an institution. And this requires a bit of history.

The evolution of the corporation

Business corporations are so commonplace today that it is easy to forget that they are a recent form of conducting business. Hundreds of civilizations over thousands of years bought, sold and traded goods and services using different laws than today's corporate law and using different trading institutions than the modern business corporations. Many of these older institutions (such as sole proprietorships, partnerships and guilds) still exist and thrive, as do the even earlier forms of trading associations based on family, the church, and other social networks. Indeed, until the 19th century "most business life continued in smaller enterprises, typically partnerships, where all the employees could be gathered in one family home."[55]

The modern corporation did not emerge from a grand plan, but evolved through a series of ad-hoc particular decisions. Sometimes these decisions were the result of lobbying or litigation by a particular corporation. At other times they were the result of government actions, as when the State of Delaware sought more incorporation revenues, or certain English kings needed money for a war.

For most of their history, corporations looked very different from what they look like today. Only in the past century did corporations gain the rights and characteristics that allowed them to become the dominant social institution of our time.

The earliest commercial organizations that looked somewhat like the modern corporation were created in the early 17th century.[56] Trading companies like the Hudson's Bay Company and the East India Company were granted royal charters permitting them to trade exclusively in certain areas. The members of these early associations were not shareholders as commonly understood today, but rather active traders who, in partnership, obtained monopoly trading rights from the Crown, often as a bargain for badly-needed loans. Some time after receiving their charter, the trading partners of the East India Company decided to pool their actual stock-in-trade, transfer it to the Company, and take shares of the Company in exchange. This created the first "joint-stock" company. This form was not legally recognized at the time, but the stockholders carried on regardless.

This shift of "company" form was very significant. What was originally a partnership organization of active traders was transformed into a corporate organization in which owners might have nothing to do with the operations of the business. Stocks of such a joint-stock company could be traded to people who didn't understand the business at all, but simply wanted to gamble on it making money for them. Eventually, the joint-stock corporate form was given formal legal recognition.

Joint-stock companies enabled the raising of greater sums of finance, as shares could be sold to a large number of people. This was important to the development of significant commercial ventures in times of colonial trade and the industrial revolution. However, the separation of ownership and management created an "agency" problem—the risk that management would seek to enrich themselves at the expense of shareholders. And there were abuses of stockholders, such as occurred in the South Sea Bubble.*

However, even then, the corporation did not possess all the characteristics we now associate with it. For instance, incorporation required the consideration of Parliament and issuance of a charter. Business owners found this time-consuming, and lobbied for automatic creation of corporations; in 1844 the English Parliament passed the *Joint Stock Companies Act*, enabling corporations to be formed by the simple act of registration.[57] This simple process has been further refined, and today, incorporation is available in Canada for a fee of $200 and a delay of five days.[58]

Even with the registration process, corporate shareholders still bore their full responsibility for the actions of the corporation they owned. They shared this feature with sole proprietorships and partnerships. After a heated public debate about the speculation that limited liability would bring, and after substantial lobbying, England's Parliament granted limited liability for corporations in 1856.[59] The same change had been made in Massachusetts in 1830, and Connecticut in 1837. In contrast, sole proprietors and partners still bear the responsibility for the actions of their firms.

Yet, citizens and their legislatures still had safeguards over this growing institution:

- corporations had carefully defined purposes in their charters; they were created to carry out particular activities and projects that were seen as serving the public interest, for example the construction of a canal, a bridge, or a road;
- corporations only were licensed to operate in particular locations;
- there were limits on the amount of capital—and thus power—corporations were entitled to accumulate;
- legislatures reviewed corporate charters regularly, and revoked those charters when corporations were not fulfilling their responsibilities.[60]

By the end of the 19th century, agitation for yet greater corporate freedom led to the removal of each and every one of these safeguards.[61] These changes, and further loosened rules on mergers and acquisitions,

* The South Sea Bubble An early example of the joint-stock company, the South Sea Company was formed in 1711. It had little prospect for success in its commercial ventures, relying on English trade in Spanish-dominated latitudes. Nonetheless South Sea Company "insiders" managed to convince a gullible public that share ownership held promise of great riches. The share price shot up in a speculative bubble, and when the inevitable crash arrived, the entire country suffered, not just the shareholders.

As an indication of the impact of the crash, several remaining directors – and the Chancellor of the Exchequer – were sent to the Tower of London. Many of the others had fled England. The policy response to the South Sea Bubble was Parliament's 1720 ban of the creation of corporations. This ban lasted over 100 years and was only lifted in 1825.

led to a rapid concentration in corporate wealth and power; in just the six years up to 1904, 1,800 corporations were consolidated into 157.[62]

* Policy competition, also known as "the race to the bottom," is the practice of jurisdictions setting policy (e.g. environmental regulations, labour standards, banking confidentiality) in order to attract and retain investment and eco-nomic activity. Delaware is an example of a jurisdiction that has used policy competition specifically in order to attract corporate registrations, shaping its corporate laws to offer the greatest corporate freedoms and lack of ac-countability. Other jurisdictions are then motivated to play catch-up and change their corporate laws accordingly in order to attract corporate regis-trations. Delaware has thus played a significant role in the development of the current corporate form, and continues to do so (recent initiatives include secrecy over the beneficial owners of corporations).

* A fuller explanation of these and other corporate characteristics is provided by the Vancouver based corporate reform agency, the Aurora Institute (www.aurora. ca).

Throughout its few hundred years of existence, the corporation has undergone several major changes. Some of these changes were made by courts, some by legislatures, some by kings, and some by shareholders and corporations themselves. There was no coherent plan in these changes, much less a consideration of the long-term public interest. These changes occurred as *ad-hoc* particular decisions.

Because our system of law is founded upon the principles of precedent and formal equality, the changes granted to a particular corporation at a particular time ended up being applicable to all corporations in the future. As policy competition* pushed jurisdictions to compete for economic activity of corporations, these changes spread from jurisdiction to jurisdiction. This process of particular, local changes spreading to all corporations and across jurisdictions continues today.

The corporation in its current form, with its current structures and characteristics, is a product of contingent, path-dependent history. There is nothing inevitable about it. The corporation has changed and continues to change, as corporate directors, legislatures, investors, and courts make ad-hoc, particular decisions based on a variety of goals and interests.

The evolutionary outcome

The evolution of the corporation to date has defined its current characteristics. These characteristics,[63] together, are what makes these institutions behave the way they do, whether it is selling flowers, automobiles or cigarettes. Just as human characteristics determine human actions (thirst, hunger, tiredness have predictable consequential behaviours) and physical characteristics will determine chemical behaviour (water predictably boils when heated), so will corporate characteristics determine the behaviour of corporations.

Three important corporate characteristics* are:

- the **imperative to maximize profits**, which restricts corporations from acting in ways that protect public health if the result is a reduction in short and long-term profits;
- the **limited liability of owners** which protects investors from having to face the consequences of corporate wrongdoing;
- the **limited accountability** of corporate directors which makes corporations accountable only to their shareholders and, in effect, only accountable for their profitability.

The profit maximization imperative

It's not just the job of directors and officers of corporations to maximize share value and profits, it is the law. A typical corporations law, Canada's federal statute [64] imposes the following duty of care on corporate directors and officers:

> 122. (1) Every director and officer of a corporation in exercising their powers and discharging their duties shall:
> (a) act honestly and in good faith with a view to the best interests of the corporation; and
> (b) exercise the care, diligence and skill that a reasonably prudent person would exercise in comparable circumstances.

Acting in the "best interests of a corporation" has been defined by courts in a very specific way to mean making the values of the shares as high as possible, or maximization the share value. [65] Share value is determined by the market, and market forces ensure that the share value reflects the perceived long and short term profitability of a corporation. Thus maximizing share value means maximizing profits.

There are other laws that also apply to corporations, such as labour codes, environmental laws and the common law. Corporations (including tobacco corporations) seek to mitigate and often violate these laws.

There is no flexibility for priority to be given to other considerations, like moral qualms, ethical concerns, community requests, or health protection over maximizing profits. The situation can be different for enterprises that are not traded, like corporations held by one shareholder (e.g. Lee Valley Tools), sole proprietorships (e.g. a family run corner store) or partnerships (like some law firms). In those cases, the owner(s) can direct the directors to take specific actions aimed at some other purpose, which may not maximize profits. But when corporations have a broad ownership, or even a small group of owners who do not agree unanimously to pursue activities at the cost of reduced profits, the law is clear: profit maximization is the overarching and sole responsibility of corporate directors.

The requirement that directors maximize share value and profits stems from the vulnerability of shareholders to the abuses created by the separation of ownership and management. This rule does help to protect shareholders from occasionally adverse financial interests of managers and directors, but it also makes corporations unable to pursue other goals that might be socially beneficial.

The impact of the profit maximization imperative is significant to public health for several reasons. It restricts the ability of individuals within a corporation to support health objectives if those objectives in any way impede profitability. Neither employees, nor managers nor directors have the legal right or ability to change the corporation's sole focus on profit, or to act contrary to the corporation's mandate to make money for its owners. Even if they wanted to, corporate directors could not lawfully engage the corporation in activities that are charitable or otherwise socially, environmentally or of public health benefit if this would mean reduction in profits.

Nor could executives or other employees do so, as they are bound by contracts to do their jobs, and corporate directors have to ensure that those jobs are aimed at profit maximization. Nor, as we will see below, could the corporations' major institutional investors do so, as they share the same legal mandates as corporations—maximizing return on the holdings of their investors.

The newsmagazine *The Economist*, in a recent review of Corporate Social Responsibility, was unequivocal about the obligations of company managers:

> *Nothing obliges someone who believes that the tobacco industry is evil to work in that industry. But if someone accepts a salary to manage a tobacco business in the interests of others, he has an obligation to those owners. To flout that obligation is unethical.* [66]

The profit maximization rule transformed corporations from organizations serving the state and public interest into machines for extracting wealth and funneling that wealth to its private shareholders, while externalizing environmental and social costs onto the public.

Limited liability

When a sole proprietor is sued, the owner of that business will be liable for the full value of the court's judgment, regardless of the value of her or his investment. Not so for corporations.

Limited liability protects owners of both publicly-traded and closely-held corporations from personal liability for the actions of the corporation that they own. Shareholders can gain unlimited returns from a corporation's activities, but do not risk losing any more than their investment in the event that the corporation is fined for committing offences, is sued for damages, or goes bankrupt.

Because of limited liability, the owners of tobacco corporations can continue to collect their share of the profits from cigarette sales without having to accept any responsibility for illness, death and the public and private costs caused by cigarettes. They are insulated from any future legal claims greater than the value of their investment.

Limited accountability

Canadian corporations are accountable through their Boards of Directors to their shareholders. They are not accountable to the general public.

Recent Wall Street and Bay Street proposals for reforms to corporate accountability in light of recent corporate scandals (Enron, WorldCom, Hollinger, and Nortel, to name just a few) aim for greater accountability to shareholders, not to the public. Quite simply, corporations are not accountable to anyone other than their shareholders.[67]

In the context of tobacco, corporations owe no allegiance or accountability to people addicted to tobacco, to children and families of sick or dead smokers, to the publicly funded health care system that spends billions of dollars per year in addressing smoking-related disease, to employers who suffer productivity losses due to employee illnesses, to the victims of second-hand smoke, or to anyone else. The creators of the anti-tobacco action *Licensed to Kill* discovered that their stated corporate purpose, "the manufacture and marketing of tobacco products in a way that each year kills over 400,000 Americans and 4.5 million other persons worldwide,"[68] was no impediment to being granted corporate status by the State of Virginia.

Even accountability to shareholders is limited; corporations are only accountable in the narrow sense of maximizing *financial* benefits to shareholders. They are not required to serve any of the other needs or interests of shareholders. As discussed above, directors are under the legal obligation to maximize profits, regardless of whether some or even all individual shareholders would prefer a corporation to take a particular course of action considered more "socially responsible." Directors of tobacco corporations are under the obligation to maximize profits, even if the extra people their corporations addict and kill are shareholders.

The hope of significantly changing corporate behaviour through shareholder resolutions is quite limited. During the mandatory annual meetings of corporations, shareholders can make votable proposals to require the directors and the corporation to carry out such a course of action. In reality, however, ownership is dispersed among thousands or millions of shareholders,[69] so it is very difficult to organize any meaningful shareholder resolutions.

The repeated attempts of health groups and other activist shareholders to change tobacco corporation behaviour illustrates the narrow scope of accountability. At the annual general meetings of tobacco corporations, shareholders frequently forward motions encouraging tobacco corporations to change their marketing behaviour.[70] These proposals are, virtually without exception, voted down. One of the reasons they are voted down is that the shares are controlled not by individual shareholders who may be willing to exercise responsible stewardship of the corporation, but by pension funds, mutual funds or other institutional investors. These institutional investors are similar to corporations themselves in being mandated to operate on the same governing principle as corporate boards: they are required to maximize unit-holder returns on investment.

The Canada Pension Plan Investment Board, for example, has codified its voting guidelines and affirmed that, when faced with issues regarding what they term "socially responsible and investing ethics" (in which they include tobacco), they will "support changes in corporate practices that are likely to enhance long-term shareholder value"[71]—i.e. long-term profits. On behalf of pension plan contributors, the CPP Investment board votes against shareholder motions aimed at improving tobacco industry actions, such as motions requiring Altria (formerly Phillip Morris) to disclose to smokers the risks of light cigarettes.[72] Serving the "best interests" of CPP contributors is interpreted only as making money for them, even if it means contributing to the death of many of them.

Predictable behaviour

Cats purr when happy. Plants turn their leaves towards the sun. Cars stop when braked. The behaviour of corporations is similarly predictable, and similarly based on the underlying programming. Just as genetic programming cues the behaviour of plants and animals and mechanical programming determines the behaviour of machines, the inherent characteristics of corporations prevail on them to behave predictably. Corporations will predictably behave (driven by the characteristics listed in parentheses) to:

- **Increase revenues (profit maximization)**
  Revenues—one half of the profit equation*—can be increased by increasing the volume of sales, selling at a higher unit price, or both. Corporations will generally raise their prices as high as the market will allow. (There are exceptions, such as price cuts aimed at harming or destroying the competition.) They will also seek to increase their sales by taking market share from their competitors and recruiting more consumers.

  * Profits equal revenue minus costs.

- **Reduce costs (profit maximization; limited liability; limited accountability)**
  Costs—the other half of the profit equation—can be reduced by increasing internal efficiency and by externalizing costs (imposing them on others). Because corporations are only accountable to their own shareholders, they will attempt where possible to impose their costs on others, rather than make their shareholders pay for them. Examples of externalized costs are the practices of disposing of wastes

into public resources, like water and air, or selling products that impose health care costs on the public purse. Limited liability shields shareholders from risks of having to pay potentially enormous costs of risky activities.

- **Influence public policy by lobbying (profit maximization)**
  The effectiveness of lobbying (or at least its perceived importance) is demonstrated by the size of the lobbyist sector. There are now over 3,000 lobbyists registered in Canada and the top ranked subject matter for lobbyists is "industry," followed by "international trade" and "taxation and finance."[73]

- **Influence public policy by litigation (profit maximization, limited liability)**
  Litigation is similarly effective, and similarly utilized by corporations. Corporations initiate far more cases under the *Charter of Rights and Freedoms* than do other groups: over five times more than Aboriginal peoples, over eight times more than labour interests, and over 10 times more than civil libertarians.[74] Again, limited liability helps shield the beneficiaries of corporate litigation—the shareholders—from court-imposed financial losses in excess of their shareholding investments.

- **Violate voluntary guidelines and laws (profit maximization, limited liability, limited accountability)**
  Corporations cannot be imprisoned, and the imprisonment of individual corporate managers or directors is extremely rare. The penalties for breaking laws is usually a fine, which a corporations can and will interpret fines as another cost to be balanced against revenues. Until very recently, fines in Canada have been tax-deductible for corporations.[75] Limited accountability means that corporations focus on maximizing profits even if it means repeatedly breaking the law; many corporations are repeat offenders, including large, familiar ones. The *Multinational Monitor* lists over 40 "major legal breaches" by General Electric between 1990 and 2001.[76] Limited liability again means that those who profit from corporate crime—the shareholders—are not exposed to losses due to criminal fines.

Tobacco corporations, as we saw earlier, have behaved in these predicted ways, and we can anticipate they will continue to do so. It is in their nature. They are "hard-wired" to behave this way. We can no more expect them to behave differently than we can ask a ball not to roll downhill.

How then, can we reprogram the tobacco industry to act differently? What would it take for them to work in ways which supported, rather than hindered, the goals of reducing smoking?

Corporate social responsibility and tobacco

One of the most current proposals to align corporate behaviour with social needs is the movement for Corporate Social Responsibility (CSR).* This is a new variant of "good corporate citizenship," "enlightened self-interest" and other similar ideas of improved corporate behavior.

There are many reasons why Corporate Social Responsibility should not and cannot be relied upon to result in tobacco corporations behaving in ways that will support the public health goals of reducing the harms associated with smoking.

Some of these reasons are theoretical. Business theorists of all stripes, ranging from Milton Friedman to Peter Drucker to Noam Chomsky, point out that corporations exist solely to maximize profits. Joel Bakan cites Milton Friedman's admonition that there is but one "social responsibility" for corporate executives—to make as much money as possible for their shareholders and Noam Chomsky's reflection that corporations' concerns must be "only for their stockholders and...not the community or the workforce or whatever."[77] If it is the legal and ethical obligation of tobacco corporation directors to make money for their shareholders, then any Corporate Social Responsibility activities must also be directed at increasing share value. Activities that improve the reputation of the corporation (like charitable donations), and thus give it more influence over public policy decisions, may be in the shareholders' interest. Activities that result in lower revenues from cigarette sales are not.

* The Conference Board of Canada describes corporate social responsibility as "the overall relationship of the corporation with all of its stakeholders. Elements of social responsibility include investment in community outreach, employee relations, creation and maintenance of employment, environmental stewardship, and financial performance." (Conference Board Press release, September 30, 2002)

The practical reasons to reject CSR as a way of improving tobacco industry behaviour have also been explored. U.K. tobacco control researchers Jeff Collin and Anna Gilmore reviewed tobacco industry initiatives in this area and found "serious questions about the social implications of the appropriation of CSR by tobacco corporations."[78] The authors reviewed the engagement of tobacco corporations in CSR initiatives, including BAT's *Social Report 2001/2002* and its donation of £3.8 million to the University of Nottingham for an International Centre for Corporate Social Responsibility. The corporations provided a similarly generous grant to University of Toronto St. Michael's College in 2004.[79] They concluded that these efforts were aimed not at achieving social objectives, but at achieving the tobacco industry objective of operating in an unregulated environment. It was, the authors decided, "a new global twist on the long-established industry tactic of voluntarily adopting ineffectual and tokenistic codes of conduct in an attempt to forestall more binding legislation."[80]

In addition to forestalling effective public health measures to reduce smoking, CSR has also been used to increases shareholder value. Hirschhorn reviewed documents from Altria/Philip Morris and traced how the corporation deliberatively engaged in corporate social responsibility activities to increase the value of its stock.[81]

At a very common-sense level, CSR cannot be expected to work with respect to tobacco. It would be quite naïve to expect tobacco corporations to help achieve social goals at the expense of profits; and it would be unlawful for their directors to allow them to do so. Tobacco corporation have the power to undertake one CSR measure that—far above and beyond all others—would have a hugely positive impact on society. They could stop selling tobacco. No tobacco corporation has proposed this, and this in itself indicates the futility of CSR as a measure to reign in tobacco corporations.

And the competitive for-profit tobacco market puts a further nail into this coffin. Even if a corporation were to voluntarily put itself out of business, there would be no social benefit, as other corporations would simply enter the market and replace that corporation's sales. CSR won't cut it; a more meaningful transformation of the tobacco industry is required.

This knowledge about corporate behavior has clear implications for public health. In the long-term, maximizing cigarette corporation shareholder value means selling more cigarettes. Tobacco corporations, if left in their current position in the industry, will continue to work to expand their markets and their sales, and to defeat, weaken and violate public health measures.

Because tobacco industry actions have been characterized as wrong, immoral and unethical, governments and public agencies have approached reforming the industry by applying the standard tools of rehabilitation and reform. Companies have been shamed (through denormalization or "truth" campaigns), punished (through law-suits) and have had codes of conduct imposed on them (like mandatory health warning labels, or advertising bans) .

If, on the other hand, tobacco industry behaviour is understood and accepted to be entirely rational and rule-driven, then different approaches to changing the industry may prove beneficial. In this second case, what is needed is a method of changing the rules that drive those that supply cigarettes. One policy instrument that could achieve this is reform of the industry itself.

We can choose how tobacco is sold

There is no reason that tobacco "has to" be sold by business corporations. There are many other institutional forms to whom the business of providing tobacco could be entrusted. We don't have to look very far to find examples of other choices we could make.

Canada, like most countries, is a mixed economy where goods and services are provided by public and private sectors, by government and non-governmental businesses, and on a profit and not-for-profit basis. Huge sectors of our economy — primary and secondary education, hospitals, public utilities, emergency services, defense, municipal infrastructures to name but a few — are dominated by organizations that are owned by and accountable to the public. Nor do we have to look far to look for examples of governments transferring ownership or direction from the private for-profit sector into public hands or from public ownership into private hands.

How a given sector of the economy is managed is the result of policy choices. Sometimes these choices are made explicitly, as when laws are passed or agreements of purchase are signed. Other times decisions are tacit, as is often the case when governments decide to remain with the status quo. The choice of business corporations as the suppliers of tobacco is one that was inherited from a time before the harmfulness of cigarettes was fully understood.

It is unlikely that the Canadian public would today choose multinational tobacco corporations to supply cigarettes if they were given a choice. In September 2004, the polling firm Environics asked Canadians which type of organization they would most trust to protect the public when it comes to distributing a product that has a known health risk. The answer suggests that those who currently supply the tobacco market would be the almost the last choice Canadians would make.

Which of the following organizations would you most trust to protect the public when it comes to distributing a product that has a known health risk? [82]

A government agency	41%
A charitable or non-profit organization	25%
An independent marketing board	19%
A multinational business corporation	5%
Don't know	7%
Some other type of organization	2%
None	1%

An instrumental choice

The decision to allow tobacco supply to continue with the existing form of tobacco corporation, or to move it to a new form of institution should not and need not be an ideological choice, but rather an instrumental one.

One of the choices we can make is to entrust this dangerous product to an institution that helps us achieve health goals (reducing smoking and the harms associated with smoking) and which also helps achieve other social goals (reducing smuggling or illegal sales). Such a choice is "instrumental" in the sense that the institution would be selected in order to achieve an identified outcome.

Canada is a mature democracy, capable of shaping her institutions in ways that meet her people's needs. Indeed, as morally responsible citizen-actors we do shape our institutions, every day, whether expressly by acting to change them or tacitly by allowing them to remain as they are. We as citizens are responsible for our institutions, and it is up to us—and only us—to define the shape of the tobacco industry and the organizations engaged in it.

The question is not whether we can reform the tobacco industry. Clearly we can. The question is what exactly we want the industry to look like. For this, we must first identify what it is that we want to achieve.

Tobacco corporations are essentially simple machines that are programmed in ways that will predictably result in their continuing attempts to increase tobacco sales, lobby and litigate to remove public health measures and violate voluntary guidelines and laws.

They have done so in the past, they continue to do so today, and they will do so in the future for as long as they exist in the tobacco supply chain. If we want to get past this behaviour, to move on to an era of a cooperative tobacco industry that helps us to reduce tobacco consumption, then we have to look at changing the very nature of the industry. If we want to have better success controlling the disease, we need to consider changing the disease vector.

THREE

Modern tobacco control strategies

When the U.S. Surgeon General[83] *2000 Report on Smoking* opened with the question "What works?" the answer provided listed educating the public, treating nicotine addiction, regulating advertising and promotion, restricting minors' access to tobacco, banning smoking in indoor places, and using taxes to keep cigarette prices high as measures which worked in isolation and which worked synergistically in combination.

These policy components are the bedrock of modern comprehensive tobacco control programs. They are recommended by the World Health Organization[84] and codified in the Framework Convention on Tobacco Control (FCTC).[85] Supporting this approach is an evidence base of the effectiveness:

- **Taxation to achieve high cigarette prices**
  A 10% price increase in excise tax is associated with reductions in tobacco consumption of 4% in high-income countries, and by 8% in low or middle-income countries.[86]

- **Advertising and promotion bans**
  "Comprehensive advertising bans do reduce cigarette consumption."[87]

- **Consumer education**
  Mass media — particularly long-term high intensity counter-advertising campaigns — prevent tobacco use initiation and increase cessation.[88]

- **Warning labels**
  Warning labels that are sufficiently noticeable deter smoking initiation and support quitting.[89]

- **Smoke-free spaces**
  Bans on smoking in public places and work places protect non-smokers from cigarette smoke and reduce both the number of smokers and the number of cigarette that remaining smokers consume.[90]

Other recommended tobacco control measures included in the FCTC (many of which are in place in Canada) are:

- **licensing** (but not restricting the number of licenses) those providing tobacco;
- **prohibition** on sales to minors;
- **regulatory authority** over the manufacture of cigarettes;
- **reporting** requirements for ingredients, emission and other product information;
- **smuggling controls** including package markings, taxing at source and posting of bonds;
- **policing powers** for inspection and investigation;
- **litigation** against tobacco companies;
- **clinical support** and training for health care professionals, etc.

The FCTC is not only the world's first modern public health treaty, it is also a disease control regime which has one of the highest levels of scientific and democratic support, having been endorsed by virtually every major health authority and unanimously agreed to by the 192 member states of the World Health Organization.[91] It reflects a broad consensus among governments, academics, non governmental organizations and professional bodies about the constituent elements of an effective comprehensive tobacco control strategy.

The goal of reducing tobacco demand (but not supply)

The comprehensive measures of the FCTC are, with the exception of minors' access laws and anti-smuggling initiatives, measures aimed at reducing people's desire to smoke, or impairing their ability to do so.

Within the paradigm of drug management, tobacco control measures usually attempt to change the behaviour of consumers (they are "demand-reduction" strategies). They do not primarily aim to control the availability of cigarettes (they are not "supply" strategies).[92]

Demand-side interventions "change the consumer"

Established tobacco control measures aim to make young persons less likely to start smoking, make smokers more willing to quit smoking, make smokers less likely to smoke in front of others, and make passive smokers more likely to protect themselves from exposure to second-hand smoke.

Even those measures aimed at corporate or institutional behaviour (such as bans on advertising or smoke-free workplace laws) have individual behaviour as their ultimate goal. They are the **means** to the **end** of reducing individuals' tobacco use. This focus on individual behaviour change is reflected in Canada's national tobacco strategy.[93]

Canada's National Strategy for Tobacco Use

Goals for a Renewed Tobacco Control Strategy
The epidemic of death and disease among Canadians resulting from tobacco use, can only be stopped by ending the use of tobacco products. It is recognized it will take several decades to achieve the vision of a smoke-free society. However, taking collaborative action can lead to significant progress toward that objective. The four goals and five strategic directions presented in this paper provide a framework for continuous and increasing efforts by governments and non-governmental organizations, individuals, health intermediaries and communities.
The four goals are:

- *Prevention*
Preventing tobacco use among young people.

- *Cessation*
Persuading and helping smokers to stop using tobacco products.

- *Protection*
Protecting Canadians by eliminating exposure to second-hand smoke.

- *Denormalization*

  Educating Canadians about the marketing strategies and tactics of the tobacco industry and the effects the industry's products have on the health of Canadians in order that social attitudes are consistent with the hazardous, addictive nature of tobacco and industry products.

There's no demand for supply-side interventions for tobacco

Tobacco control measures have tried to change the **business practices** of tobacco companies (i.e. marketing practices) but have not tried to change the core **business principles** under which the companies operate (i.e. in competition, or with the intention of making money). Nor have they sought to change the **economic principles** of the tobacco market. Under lax tobacco control regimes as under strict tobacco control regimes, tobacco companies continue to pursue profits and these profits are associated with continued (or increased) sales of cigarettes. Tobacco companies operate increasingly in a free and globalizing market (one with few national boundaries, tariff or import barriers).

The World Bank is particularly unfriendly towards supply-side interventions. In its widely distributed set of policy recommendations, *Curbing the Epidemic*, it counsels "While interventions to reduce demand for tobacco are likely to succeed, measures to reduce its supply are less promising."[94] Yet only two supply-side interventions are commonly implemented to reduce smoking—restrictions on sales to minors, and smuggling controls. The first of these is increasingly viewed as being ineffective.[95] Excluded from the list of potential measures are supply controls which are commonly used by governments to manage different commodities and services, measures such as restrictions on the number of licensees, tariff barriers, import restrictions, government controlled monopolies, etc.

Respected economists in tobacco control are unambiguous on this point. Canadian health economist, Prabhat Jha, expressed the view:

> While interventions to reduce the demand for tobacco are likely to succeed, measures to reduce its supply usually fail. Attempts to impose restrictions on the sale of cigarettes to youths in high income countries have mainly been unsuccessful. Moreover, in low-income

countries it may be difficult to implement and enforce such restric-tions. Crop substitution is often proposed as a means to reduce the tobacco supply, but there is little evidence that it reduces consump-tion, since the incentives for farmers to grow tobacco are currently much greater than for most other crops.

The evidence suggests that freer trade in tobacco products has led to increases in smoking and other tobacco use. Because trade restrictions impose other costs, a better option is for countries to adopt measures that effectively reduce demand and apply those measures equally to imported and domestically produced ciga-rettes.

However, one supply side measure is vital action against smug-gling. Effective measures include prominent tax stamps and local language warnings on cigarette packs, as well as the aggressive en-forcement of anti-smuggling measures and consistent application of tough penalties to deter smugglers. [96]

Approved or not, supply-side tobacco measures are plentiful in Canada

Examples of supply-side interventions affecting tobacco that have been employed in Canada include transition payments for tobacco farmers,[97] import tariffs on tobacco to protect the domestic tobacco market, anti-smuggling initiatives, bans on sales to minors, bans on vending machines, controls on foreign investment, limits on market share to ensure compe-tition.[98] The requirement of the Competition Bureau that BAT divest its holdings in Rothmans, Benson & Hedges to ensure competition in the cigarette market was another supply-side intervention.

Recent legislation banning youth possession (and not only banning sales-to-youth) of cigarettes in Nova Scotia and Alberta[99] is another sup-ply-side intervention.

The Ontario Flue-Cured Tobacco Growers' Marketing Board is an example of government endorsing (through legislation) a supply-side intervention designed to assist tobacco farmers. So is the recently-an-nounced Canadian government program to provide $71 million in aid to tobacco farmers in the form of transition payments)[100] for Canadian to-bacco farmers, and the proposal of the Council for a Tobacco-Free Prince

Edward Island and the Canadian Cancer Society for a tobacco sales to be restricted to liquor-store style outlets.[101]

Other approaches to managing tobacco

Just as there is a vast Canadian experience in transforming industries to achieve public goals, there is a vast global experience in transforming the tobacco industry. To date, government interventions in the industry have usually been intended to protect trade, and have had the result—intended or otherwise—of increasing sales. With a better understanding of the devastating health impacts of tobacco use, it is likely that governments will be willing to intervene to protect public health, not to mention public budgets, a likelihood borne out by at least one example to date.

With the goal of increasing competition, governments have dissolved tobacco monopolies and oligopolies

EXAMPLE One of the most noteworthy early examples was the U.S. government application of the *Sherman Anti-trust Act* in 1911 to break up the American Tobacco Corporation, which, at that time, controlled 97% of the U.S. market and 92% of the global cigarette market.[102]

More recent interventions with similar effect were encouraged by the International Monetary Fund and other international economic agencies. These were imposed on newly industrialized economies following the lifting of the iron curtain in the late 1980s, and on Asian countries following the Asian economic crisis a decade later. In those two decades, almost 70,000 state-owned tobacco enterprises were privatized,[103] primarily those in the former Soviet Union and Asia.

EXAMPLE At the time British American Tobacco and Rothmans International merged operations in January 1999, their combined market share of the Canadian tobacco market was 88%. The Canadian Competition Bureau decided "the merger would result in a substantial lessening or prevention of competition from a lack of effective alternatives or import competition, high levels of concentration and high barriers. As a result,

BAT sold all of the assets acquired in Rothmans in Canada by February 2000.[104]

With the goal of maintaining domestic control of tobacco revenues, countries have created cigarette monopolies

In more than a dozen countries, state tobacco monopolies are the leading providers of cigarettes, with an aggregate global market share of 40%.[105]

EXAMPLE The world's largest tobacco corporation, the China National Tobacco Company (CNTC) is state-owned and managed,[106] and an important part of that government's operations. Tobacco sales provide the Chinese government with 10% of its revenues, compared with less than 1% of government revenues in OECD countries.[107] China's tobacco market was not always state-run: in 1939, British American Tobacco had over 50% market share (and its Chinese sales produced 25% of BAT's profits).[108]

With the goal of competing against privatized corporations in newly liberalized markets, governments have privatized or semi-privatized their state-monopolies

EXAMPLE Japan Tobacco was a state-monopoly until 1994, when it the process began of transferring it into private management and ownership in order to compete more effectively for market share against newly imported U.S. cigarettes. Having acquired the global operations of a RJR-Nabisco in 1999, Japan Tobacco is now the world's third largest tobacco manufacturer outside of China. The government of Japan continues, by law, to own between 30% and 50% of its shares.[109]

With the goal of stabilizing farm income, governments have applied supply-management to tobacco growing

EXAMPLE The Ontario Flue-Cured Tobacco Growers' Marketing Board is an example of government endorsing (through legislation) a market intervention designed to assist tobacco farmers. So is the recently-announced Canadian government program to provide $71 million in aid to tobacco farmers in the form of transition payments).[110]

With the goal of protecting public health, governments have defended a variety of market interventions against trade challenges

EXAMPLE In a 1990 GATT hearing, Thailand defended its tobacco monopoly and other market interventions on the grounds that they were necessary to protect health. Although Thailand lost the battle to maintain its complete ban on all tobacco imports, it won the war, with the GATT panel refusing to rule against its import taxes; tax preference for cheaper cigarettes (i.e. domestic cigarettes); distribution channels controlled by the Thai Tobacco Monopoly; and limits on domestic production by foreign firms.[111]

With the goal of ensuring competition, governments have restricted private ownership of tobacco companies

EXAMPLE At the time British American Tobacco and Rothmans International merged operations in January 1999, their combined market share of the Canadian tobacco market was 88%. The Canadian Competition Bureau decided "the merger would result in a substantial lessening or prevention of competition from a lack of effective alternatives or import competition, high levels of concentration and high barriers. As a result, BAT sold all of the assets acquired in Rothmans in Canada by February 2000.[112]

EXAMPLE Although it has liberalized its cigarette manufacturing operations, France has maintained a monopoly over cigarette distribution. French tobacco retailers (*les buralistes* or *bureaux de tabac*) have exclusive rights to sell tobacco for a specified period in a specific area, granted by the French tax office (*Administration des Douanes et des Droits Indirects*).[113] There are fewer retailers selling tobacco in France than in Canada (34,000[114] compared with 40,000[115]) for a population of smokers roughly twice as large.

With the goal of reducing smoking, one country has moved towards banning cigarette sales

EXAMPLE A unique supply-side intervention designed to reduce tobacco use is found in Bhutan, where tobacco sales have been banned in 19 of 20 subnational districts.[116]

"Why don't we just ban tobacco?"

The reluctance of health advocates, academics and government officials to plan the end of smoking is not necessarily shared by the Canadian public, many of whom ask "why don't we just *ban* tobacco!?"

There are very few people with the power to make it happen who are willing to ban tobacco. Although the House of Commons recommended a ban on cigarettes a century ago,[117] neither on that occasion nor any since has a government proposed doing so.

Health authorities are quite firmly against banning tobacco. The current experience with illicit drugs, like cannabis and cocaine, suggests that prohibition causes more problems than it solves by increasing criminal activity.[118] Past experience with alcohol suggests that bans may reduce use, but are not likely to actually eliminate it. Furthermore, bans may not achieve the intended purpose of reducing disease.

Making a substance illegal without being able to make it unused increases the lack of consumer protection for harmful substances. The illegal market for marijuana, for example, does not allow government to require health warning labels on marijuana when it is sold, to ensure that it is supplied in ways that allow for less harmful (i.e. non-smoked) use, or oversee manufacture. Using criminal law power to manage a health problem (addiction) contributes to the social marginalization (some would say victimization) of those who need help.

The World Bank provides a useful summary of the often-repeated arguments against prohibition:

> [T]he prohibition of tobacco is unlikely to be either feasible or effective. First, even when substances are prohibited, they continue to be widely used, as is the case with many illicit drugs. Second, prohibition creates its own sets of problems: it is likely to increase criminal activity and entail costly police enforcement. Third, from an economic perspective, optimal tobacco consumption is not zero.* Fourth, the prohibition of tobacco is unlikely to be politically acceptable in most countries.[119]

* The World Bank does not provide an estimate of what the optimal level of tobacco consumption is, or why they have taken a different view from the widely held view that there is no safe level of smoking.

Nonetheless, on rare occasions, reputable health leaders have expressed support for banning tobacco. The current U.S. Surgeon General Richard H. Carmona told the House Energy and Commerce subcommittee in June 2003 that he "would support banning or abolishing tobacco products...I see no need for any tobacco products in society."[120] The White House quickly distanced itself from these comments, as did the leading U.S. anti-smoking group, Tobacco Free Kids.[121] Similarly, when the respected medical journal, *The Lancet*, proposed prohibition of tobacco in a strongly written editorial ("We call on Tony Blair's government to ban tobacco"),[122] the call was rejected by many in the tobacco control community. The head of U.K. anti-smoking group ASH said: "A legal ban on smoking is neither possible nor desirable. We want to help and encourage people not to smoke, not to force them."[123]

In only one country, Bhutan, has tobacco been banned.[124] Bhutan imposes the ban only on its own citizens; foreign nationals are allowed to use cigarettes.

Despite the absence of any proposals from governments or health agencies for the banning of cigarette, the idea of banning generates some public interest and support. One survey indicated that one in five Ontario adults recently supported banning the sale of tobacco products[125] as did 80% of never-smoking and 11% of current smoking teenagers.[126] This young generation of Canadians, raised in an environment where public smoking is not "normal" and where tobacco promotions are severely restricted, may be more willing than their parents' generation to entertain the idea of a tobacco-free society. Even some smokers say that they would welcome a ban as it would help them to quit (three in five smokers are planning to quit in the next six months).[127]

Leading Canadian tobacco researcher, Roberta Ferrence, recently wrote that consideration of ending the commercial supply of tobacco should not be dismissed out-of-hand.

> *Along with policies of selective discouragement, let us include bans on commercial supply as one of a range of potential tobacco control strategies that we should seriously entertain.*[128]

She notes that widespread prohibition does exist for one form of tobacco product, namely smokeless tobacco. Countries with diverse political and cultural structures have banned some form of oral tobacco product, including the European Union, Israel, Hong Kong, Singapore, New Zealand, Norway and Saudi Arabia.[129]

We may be able to phase out tobacco use without prohibiting it

Proposals to end tobacco use may have to overcome the negative (and arguably unfair) association with "tobacco prohibition." The spectre of prohibition has been employed by tobacco corporations and their apologists[130] to confuse the concept of "ending tobacco use" with "banning tobacco products."

There are a number of ways in which undesirable or no-longer-desired disappear from the market place — not all involving legal prohibitions.

Prohibition is sometimes effective, sometimes not.

History suggests that prohibition is a very poor way of ending the use of alcohol and recreational drugs, but there are some harmful goods that have been very effectively removed through regulatory bans. *The Hazardous Products Act* bans the sale of urea formaldehyde insulation[131] and Health Canada has banned the sale of baby walkers[132] without any apparent increase in the criminal supply of baby-goods or home insulation. Asbestos is not banned in Canada (although it is in France), but consumer products made with asbestos are.[133]

On the other hand, such prohibitions may be successful because of particular circumstances, such as good substitutes, shallow cultural embeddedness, and a history of sales only in reputable retail outlets. As noted above, ineffective prohibitions may increase harm.

Some products are restricted to selected individuals or occasions.

There are other products whose widespread use is not socially desired, but for which total bans are not considered desirable. In Canada, hand guns and certain pesticides may only be used by permitted categories of use or users (such as policemen or farmers), fireworks can only be used on certain days of the year, and some pharmaceuticals may only be sold when an intermediary has provided permission/prescription. Some drugs with harm potential, like methadone, can only be used under strict supervision.

Some products are actively discouraged.

There are a number of products for sale in Canada, the use of which is formally discouraged by government, but which are neither illegal nor restricted. Tobacco products currently fall into this category, as do some other consumer products, such as kava.[134]

Some products disappear on their own.

A number of products once common place in Canada are now rarely bought or sold, often because they have been replaced by superior "substitutable goods." The straight razor, for example, has largely disappeared, and has been replaced by the safety razor or electric razor. The typewriter has been replaced by computers. The apocryphal buggy-whip has been replaced by the steering wheel and accelerator pedal.

Even legal, addictive and dangerous drugs can disappear without governmental or deliberate social intervention. Many products that were once popular or that are popular elsewhere, including tobacco products, are extinct or nearly so without ever having been made illegal. These include paan, khat, plug tobacco, twist tobacco, hubble-bubble, and tobacco hookah. A century ago, pipes and nasal snuff were tobacco products commonly for sale in Canada, but these are now effectively extinct. Through consecutive market shifts, they were displaced by the evolving cigarette (initially hand-rolled, then machine-made, then filtered, then ventilated). Ironically, the pipes and nasal snuff that were displaced by the modern cigarette are considered by many to be much less likely to harm the smoker than the modern cigarette.

FOUR

Better alternatives to supply tobacco products

If tobacco must be sold, there is no reason that it must be sold by business corporations.

There are business forms other than the for-profit business corporation available to societies who do not wish to criminalize or penalize the use of tobacco, but who also wish to remove the corporate behaviour that impedes reducing the problems that tobacco causes. There are more choices than "banning tobacco" or "free-enterprise."

Collectively, we have the choice about how cigarettes are sold. Citizens, through their democratically elected governments, have the right and the power to reform any industry. We can choose a tobacco industry that works to support and promote health protection measures instead of one which undermines them.

The traditional dichotomy (public sector enterprise vs. private sector enterprise)

Tradition tells us that the fundamental economic dichotomy in our society is between the public sector and the private sector. This orthodoxy is repeated in our newspapers and our textbooks, by political commentators and party spin-doctors, by TV and radio reporters, and by bureaucrats and elected leaders in business and government. Indeed, this traditional dichotomy is stated so often that it is accepted uncritically without explanation. Thus it is useful to give it an explanation.

The public sector is generally considered to be government, in all its manifestations. Whether engaged in its legislative function (representative deliberation and the passage of laws and bylaws), or in its executive and administrative functions (regulation-making, implementing laws and regulations, fact-finding, providing services or operative businesses), a wide variety of government activities are lumped together as the "public sector." With this range of activity, it is obvious that the term "public sector" contains more differences than it demarcates.

Similarly, the term "private sector" is somewhat indeterminate. It is often used to refer to businesses. The private sector would thus include transnational, publicly-traded oil corporations, the sole proprietor barbershop, and legal and accounting partnerships ranging from two people in a small town to thousands in office towers around the world.

However, its dichotomous relationship to "public sector" suggests that the "private sector" may be any businesses that operate outside of government.* This blurs important differences between business corporations and other private sector businesses forms. For example, a credit union like VanCity[135] that operates independently of government could be considered "private sector," as could a consumer co-operative like Mountain Equipment Co-op.[136] Similarly, a non-profit or charity retailer like Goodwill[137] might be considered private sector. Just as with "public sector," the term "private sector" obscures a lot of important differences.

When it comes to business enterprises, the public sector / private sector orthodoxy actually ignores a vital, and much more interesting, dichotomy. This is a dichotomy that underpins the main thrust of this book—the dichotomy between public *interest* enterprises and private *interest* enterprises.

* In recent years the voluntary sector has been identified as a "third sector."

The interesting *dichotomy (public interest enterprise vs. private interest enterprise)*

The term "private interest enterprise" identifies the most important characteristic of a for-profit business corporation: its purpose. As discussed in Chapter 2 the sole purpose of a corporation is to make money for its shareholders. A corporation can be considered a type of investment property owned by its shareholders in order to generate dividends and capital value for them. This is their private "interest" in the corporation.

Clearly a for-profit business corporation fits into both "private" molds; it is both a private *sector* enterprise and a private *interest* enterprise. Some of the other private sector enterprises clearly are not private interest. Co-operatives, credit unions and non-profit or charity businesses are not private interest enterprises. They operate with a view to serving a larger social purpose, whether that is the alleviation of poverty, protection of the environment, or the promotion of the interests of their members and their community. Their members are not necessarily entitled to dividend payouts and the capital value upon sale of the enterprise. Thus,

Private vs. Public
Interests and Sectors

	PRIVATE	
Business corporations		
Sole proprietorships	*INTEREST*	
Other for-profit enterprise		
	SECTOR	
PRIVATE		PUBLIC
Co-operatives		Public utilities
Community interest corporations		Crown corporations
Other not-for-profit enterprise		Government services
	PUBLIC	

their members do not have the same financial "interest" in the organization as the owners of a for-profit corporation have.

Similarly, publicly-owned businesses generally operate not solely for profit, but rather for some additional or alternative purpose deemed to be in the broader public interest. There are different ways for publicly-owned businesses to be structured, including Crown corporations, government departments, and arms-length boards. They all share with co-operatives, credit unions and non-profit or charity businesses the feature of being "public interest."

Arguably there are some public sector agencies that, on the surface at least, appear to operate for private interests. But even public agencies that invest in private sector enterprises (like the Atlantic Canada Opportunities Agency) are generally doing so for a stated public purpose.

A challenging example for the public-private interest model we present are the existing state tobacco monopolies (like the Thai Tobacco Monopoly, Turkey's Tekel, Japan Tobacco or the Chinese National Tobacco Corporation). These public agencies operate in the public interest, in that they serve to increase revenues for public purposes.

Japan Tobacco (which is 50% owned by the government of Japan) has a global operation which includes JTI-Macdonald in Canada. Outside of Japan, its operations appear indistinguishable from other private sector tobacco multinationals. Being half-owned by the government of Japan has not appeared to dilute the harms it causes. In their foreign sales, this state-owned enterprise can perhaps be understood to be serving the private interest of the Japanese treasury.

As is clear from even this brief discussion there are a number of similarities between public interest enterprises and private interest enterprises. It is fair to say that the "interest" category contains a lot of distinctions, perhaps as many as the "sector" category. However, there are two vital differences between public interest enterprises and private interest enterprises — differences that explain tobacco industry behaviour to date, and point the way forward for a tobacco manufacturer that could help promote public health, instead of promoting tobacco consumption.

As noted above, in many areas public interest enterprises are very similar to private interest enterprises. Looking at them from the outside, one might not immediately perceive any difference, as they can resemble private interest enterprises in many ways, including:

- **Structure**
Public interest enterprises are comprised of members or shareholders who elect a board of directors that in turn supervises the people who carry out the operations (employees, contractors and volunteers).

- **Legal characteristics**
Public enterprises generally obtain federal or provincial registration. Either one gives them important abilities to carry out a commercial undertaking, including limited liability, "perpetual succession" or immortality (i.e. they continue to exist when key personnel leave or die, unlike a sole proprietorship or small partnership), the capacity to enter into contracts, and the capacity to sue and be sued.

- **Tangible operations and assets**
A public interest enterprise can have any of the visible trappings of any business, whether they be: plants, warehouses, storefronts and trucks; or offices, cubicles, computers and water coolers.

- **Size**
Public interest enterprises come in a range of sizes. Like small for-profit businesses, some public interest enterprises are small, entrepreneurial one-person operations. Like large corporations, some public interest enterprises are large, managerial organizations with national or international operations.

- **Environment**
Like corporations, public interest enterprises work in all sorts of environments, from lightly regulated (e.g. consumer products) to carefully regulated (e.g. medical services), from monopoly (e.g. some agricultural marketing organizations) to oligopoly (e.g. financial services) to competitive market (e.g. retail sales).

- **Functional capacity**

  Public interest enterprises take on a variety of roles in an economy, in a variety of ways, at a variety of scales. There is no function that they cannot take on in theory, and probably very few functions that they haven't already taken on in practice.

Public and private interest enterprises — key differences

Despite the above-noted similarities, public interest enterprises differ from private interest enterprises in two fundamentally important and related areas.

- **The motives and the accountability of the public interest enterprise are completely different from those of the private interest enterprise.**

  As we saw earlier, the for-profit business corporation is required to maximize profits for its shareholders. If the directors of a corporation were to sacrifice profits to advance some other cause, they would be in jeopardy of being sued, as Henry Ford was sued by his brother-in-law.* This strictly private interest mandate is the motivation for the decisions of the corporation.

- **The accountability of a corporation is solely to its shareholders.**

  The corporation owes no duty to anyone or anything other than its shareholders.

  For public interest enterprises, the story is on both counts different.

* When Henry Ford attempted to keep car prices down to levels where most working people could afford to purchase a car, he was successfully sued by his brother-in-law, a shareholder. His brother in law, Mr. Dodge, took the proceeds of the suit to form his own car company. (Dodge v. Ford Motor Company, 1919).

Public interest corporations

As discussed public interest enterprises can be in either the public or private sector: they are not all owned by government. Some, like co-operatives and non-profit businesses, are owned by individuals or organized members. These familiar government and non-governmental models, as well as more recent proposals, provide interesting lessons for how we might choose to create a health-promoting tobacco manufacturer.

Co-operatives

A co-operative is a business owned and controlled by its member patrons and operated for them and by them. In general, co-operatives are guided by a set of seven principles: 1) voluntary and open membership; 2) democratic member control; 3) member economic participation; 4) autonomy and independence; 5) education, training, and information; 6) co-operation among co-operatives; and 7) concern for community.[138]

These principles do not hinder co-operatives from being significant economic players. They are active in a number of sectors from agriculture to financial services, from outdoor gear to automobile sharing. Desjardins Group[139] and Mountain Equipment Co-op[140] are two examples of familiar and successful Canadian co-operative businesses. There are now over 10,000 co-operatives and credit unions operating in Canada[141] holding combined assets of $167 billion, and employing over 160,000 Canadians.[142] Internationally, co-operatives are even more successful. The manufacturing group of the Mondragon Corporacion Co-operative had total sales of over 4 billion Euros in 2003.[143] Co-operatives "employ more people around the world than all the multinational corporations put together."[144]

Motives of co-operatives

The co-operative's purposes include meeting the needs of its member-patrons and, unlike the corporation, the needs of the community.[145] The needs of a co-operative's member-patrons are defined more broadly than the interests of shareholders are defined in corporate law; the needs of member-patrons of a co-operative are generally considered as common needs, and both economic and social needs. In contrast, corporate shareholders' interests are considered to be solely the maximization of financial return on investment. Co-operatives thus have a much richer set of motives than corporations have.

Excesses of co-operative revenues over expenses are distributed to members and the community in a number of ways. For example, VanCity

Credit Union, based in Vancouver, distributes dividends to members and also provides grants to organizations working on environmental issues, women's shelters, the arts and many other areas. Co-operative dividends can be paid out in a variety of ways — for instance equally to all members, or on the basis of the amount of activity a member-user has with the co-operative.

Accountability of co-operatives

As with a corporation, employees of a co-operative are accountable to the board of directors, which is accountable to the member-shareholders. In a co-operative, however, member voting power is not determined by how many shares are owned. Instead, each member has one vote. The "one member, one vote" system is more democratic, in contrast to the corporation's "one share, one vote," which could be termed more "dollarcratic."

Co-operative accountability extends beyond merely that owed to the member. As noted above, purposes of co-operatives include meeting the needs of the community. The inclusion of education, training and information and co-operation among co-operatives as underlying principles further broadens the set of stakeholders to which a co-operative is accountable.

Non-profit businesses

Non-profit organizations (NPOs) are even more similar to for-profit corporations than co-operatives are. Reflecting the similarity, federally-registered non-profits are even termed "corporations" in the statute under which they are registered.[146] The key distinction between non-profit and for-profit corporations is that non-profits must not be operated for the financial gain of their members.

Non-profit organizations are not to be mistaken for charities, although they and certain other types of organizations can apply for charitable status. (Charitable status is limited to organizations that have a purpose falling within a very specific, limited, ancient court-interpreted definition of what is charitable.)[147]

Motives of non-profit organizations

Non-profit organizations have purposes stated in their constitutions. These purposes can be almost anything (they are not restricted to certain spheres of activity as charities are). Examples include protecting the environment, collecting memorabilia, or conducting research. What the purposes cannot include is making a profit and distributing it to the organization's members.

These organizations can and do engage in businesses. Often called "social enterprises" because their function is to help the organization fulfill its social mandate, the businesses run by non-profits must be subordinate to the stated purposes of the organization.[148]

The formation of social enterprises is on the rise in recent years as many non-profits have experienced reduced funding from traditional sources. Financial institutions and other organizations have been developing social enterprise capacity-building and support programs. Federal legislation proposed in the recent Throne Speech (discussed later in this chapter) could assist in accelerating the development of many social enterprises.

Accountability of non-profit organizations

As with corporations and co-operatives, non-profit employees are accountable to the board of directors, which is accountable to the members. Member voting rights are akin to those of co-operatives and not corporations; there is one vote per member. The role of the members of a non-profit is similar in most ways to that of the shareholders of a corporation, except that they would not receive any dividends or beneficially own any financial interest in the organization. Upon winding up or dissolution, non-profits generally transfer assets to another organization with a similar mandate. This is a strictly enforced requirement for those which have charitable status.[149] Like co-operatives, non-profits have a further level of accountability—to their purposes. They are required to specify their purposes and are required to comply with them. Unlike corporations, they cannot have a general purpose that allows them to carry out any activity.

Additional accountability is placed upon charities, which must report annually to the Canada Revenue Agency (formerly Revenue Canada).

Should charities step outside of their mandate, or spend more than 10% of their revenues on political activity or any revenues whatsoever on partisan political activity, the can lose their charitable status. Corporations, in contrast, are free to spend millions on lobbying and advertising relating to election issues, and are free to make donations to political parties and their supporting think tanks, and obtain *favourable* tax treatment in return.

Publicly-owned enterprises: government departments and Crown corporations

Governments can provide any range of services and products. Current or recent examples of government enterprises include water utilities, liquor distribution, petroleum products, waste collection and disposal, education, small business planning and support services, electricity, export development financing, and roads. Governments could do more: there is no legal impediment to their undertaking any (or even all) business activities in an economy.

Canada is a "mixed economy," involving both the private and public sector in many industries. Some Canadian public enterprises have participated in areas traditionally served by government, such as postal services and utilities. Others have participated in areas more traditionally served by private commercial organizations. An example of the latter was Petro-Canada, a publicly owned oil corporation established to serve the public interest through establishing government presence in, and insight into, the petroleum sector.

Crown corporations, like private-sector, private interest enterprises, are capable of managing large and complex businesses. Hydro Quebec controls assets of over $57billion,[150] more than nine times the total assets of Imperial Tobacco Canada, the largest of the Canadian "Big Three" tobacco manufacturers and in control of over 57% of total market share.[151] Canada Post employs approximately 70,000[152] people—50 times the number employed by Imperial Tobacco Canada.[153]

For the past two decades Canadian governments have followed the trend toward privatization of government enterprises, perhaps driven by the prevailing political trends, trade regimes and increased policy competition among countries. Consequently there is currently a declining level of public participation in the Canadian economy. The federal government sold the public's control over Petro-Canada to the private sector, despite the profits it was generating and the tax burden it was thus relieving. Despite this, there is still significant public participation in the Canadian economy. Even in the United States and other countries where the prevalent political mood is against government involvement in the economy, some sectors retain very heavy government participation.

Governments have at their disposal a range of systems of administering businesses, including direct administration through ministries of the Crown, and more "arms-length" administration through agencies, boards, commissions, "special operating agencies,"[154] and Crown corporations. The following sections briefly discuss two examples from opposite ends of the spectrum of control and accountability: government ministries and Crown corporations.

Motives of publicly-owned enterprises

Unlike corporations, publicly-owned enterprises generally do not have the freedom to engage in any business they like but are required to conform to the stated purposes.

The purposes of government ministries are stated in legislation and are re-stated in mission statements, strategic plans, operational plans, business plans, and the like. Cabinet, the opposition parties, the Auditor General, the media and ultimately the voters ensure that Ministries do not waver far. And in some circumstances the courts can review and reverse the actions of ministry decision-makers that go outside of their stated purposes.

Likewise, the purposes of Crown corporations are stated in their enabling legislation. These vary tremendously: some lend themselves to net revenue generation, some to break-even/cost recovery, and others to providing their goods or services at a net cost.

Other publicly-owned institutions similarly have stated purposes, including social, environmental or government revenue goals. One commonly used example is provincial liquor monopolies.[155] *

* After prohibition ended, the public sector took over distribution of alcohol. The Liquor Control Board of Ontario, for instance, was formed with a dual mandate: regulation of the sale of liquor in order to protect society, and generation of revenues for government through profits and taxes on the sale of alcohol.

Accountability of publicly-owned enterprises

There is a range of accountability mechanisms for government-adminis-tered enterprises. A closer degree of control and more direct accountabil-ity to the public can be obtained by situating a business directly under a ministry. Each government ministry has a Minister, beneath whom there is a Deputy Minister (a civil servant, as opposed to an elected leader), beneath whom there are Assistant Deputy Ministers, Directors, and so on. Thus there is a direct chain of command leading from a politician to the operational level of the Ministry, which could include a commercial enterprise. The parliamentary principle of Ministerial responsibility pro-vides accountability running up the chain of command. This principle, combined with scrutiny by Cabinet, opposition parties, the Auditor Gen-eral, the media and the voters usually tempers the will of a politician to exercise direct control over sensitive operational level decisions of a Ministry. Exceptions do occur, and scandals are occasionally reported in the media.

More common for public enterprise is the Crown corporation, which is further toward the "independent" end of the spectrum. Here, the po-tential for direct involvement in day-to-day operational decisions is fur-ther reduced, and thus traditional parliamentary accountability mecha-nisms are altered. Nonetheless there is still significant accountability to the public. Essentially the citizens of Canada, through the Minister, are the shareholders of the Crown corporation. Accountability flows from the Crown corporation's board of directors to Parliament or the provin-cial legislature via the relevant Minister, and thence to the public. The board of directors functions in much the same way as any other corpo-rate board—hiring the management and holding them accountable to the purposes of the business. However, the directors of a Crown corpora-tion are additionally required to take into account the policy direction of the citizens' elected government, not just the consumption impulses of domestic or foreign customers. In addition to appointing the board, the government approves the Crown corporation's long-term plans, and can issue directives to it (through Parliament or some other such transparent channel). As the shareholder, the Minister responsible for the Crown cor-poration is ultimately accountable in Parliament. Parliament approves the budgets of most Crown corporations, and Parliamentary Committees review their operations.

Innovative options

Community interest corporations

New public interest enterprise forms are emerging and governments are proposing new models for public interest enterprises. The United Kingdom recently created the Community Interest Company (CIC), a business form that will come into existence in the summer of 2005.[156]

The CIC was "designed for social enterprises that want to use their profits and assets for the public good"[157] and is intended to be "suitable for those who wish to work within the relative freedom of the familiar limited company framework without either the private profit motive or charity status."[158] The CIC would be similar to a for-profit business corporation in many respects that are commercially advantageous: member-elected board structure; limited liability; perpetual succession; and the capacities to contract, sue and be sued. It would have the capacity to access debt and other forms of commercial finance.[159]

However, because of its public interest orientation, a "profit and asset lock" would prohibit CICs from distributing their assets or surpluses to their members. A limited exception to the profit and asset lock would enable a CIC to obtain dividend-paying equity finance in some circumstances.[160] And the profit and asset lock itself, along with other features such as increased accountability through reporting to the regulator, will provide advantages in accessing social investment and capital from long-term investors (i.e. not high-risk, venture speculators).[161] Finally, the CIC would be able to receive grants and donations for which corporations normally would not qualify.[162]

Like the public-interest enterprises discussed above, the CIC would differ from the for-profit business corporation in two major respects: motivations and accountability.

Motives of Community Interest Companies

Community Interest Companies "will be organizations pursuing social objectives" and must pass a "community interest test" by satisfying a regulator that its purposes could be regarded by a reasonable person as being in the community or wider public interest.[163] Annual filing of a "community interest report,"[164] along with the asset and profit lock, would ensure that these purposes are adhered to.

Accountability of Community Interest Companies

These new business will be accountable not only to their members but also, through the regulator, to the wider public. The regulator would be responsible for ensuring stakeholder involvement in activities and community satisfaction. If unsatisfied with the findings, the regulator would have the "ability to change the directors or wind up the company."[165]

Other developments

Canada's federal government announced in its October 5, 2004 Throne Speech that it would establish a new *Not-for-Profit Corporations Act*, aimed at supporting activities and enterprises that benefit the community: "The Government is determined to foster the social economy—the myriad not-for-profit activities and enterprises that harness civic and entrepreneurial energies for community benefit right across Canada. The Government will help to create the conditions for their success, including the business environment within which they work."[166] Bill C-21 was introduced November 15, 2004.[167]

Other countries are moving in the same direction. In Germany a recent Parliamentary Committee recommended a review of not-for-profit purposes with a view to widening the current scope of recognized activities.[168] New regulations introduced by the Italian government in the 1990s led to a dramatic growth in the Italian social enterprise sector.[169] Spanish laws were altered in 1995 to allow not-for-profit organizations to attract greater capital investment by issuing equity shares.[170] The

Swedish government is gathering information and forming recommendations for the development of new forms for social enterprises where assets are protected for the community and company's benefit.[171]

The CIC or the not-for-profit corporation might become useful models for a health-promoting tobacco manufacturer. The details of these models would need to be finalized before this could be determined. Nonetheless, the emergence of proposals in the United Kingdom, Canada and European countries indicates that governments accept the idea that commercial enterprises can, and sometimes should, be operated in the public interest, as distinct from the private interest. The continued evolution of commercial enterprise could involve a pragmatic, instrumental re-alignment of various industry sectors to achieve public interest goals in addition to private interest goals.

Reflections on private interest vs. public interest enterprises

The public interest — private interest enterprise dichotomy is useful in the context of discussion about the tobacco industry because it highlights two organizational characteristics that strongly determine tobacco corporation behaviour: **corporate motives** and **accountability structures**.

The motives and accountability structures of public interest enterprises differ substantially from those of the private interest enterprises, including current tobacco corporations; they enable the enterprise to select, work toward and achieve an entirely different set of goals. Instead of pursuing profits, a public interest tobacco manufacturer could have purposes of supplying the market while working to *decrease*, instead of increase, consumption. It could work to support, and not undermine, public health measures. The set of existing and proposed public interest enterprises provide useful models for what a health-promoting tobacco manufacturer could look like.

The set of policy instruments used to date in tobacco control is limited. It has achieved some successes, but not enough. A wider range of policy instruments has been used in other health-related and non health-related sectors. Instruments that alter the supply chain can have both supply-side and demand-side impacts on tobacco consumption.

One potential such instrument is the reforming of the supply chain to serve the public interest, instead of private interests. Large scale commercial undertakings are successfully managed both in Canada and abroad by public-interest enterprises. Existing and proposed public interest enterprise structures contain models that would be useful in designing a tobacco manufacturer that served to promote public health rather than compromise it.

The following chapter will discuss in greater detail what such a tobacco manufacturer could look like, and how we could get there.

More on corporate choices

Lessons from other sectors

Canada is rich in examples of how to manage industrial sectors for the public good.

Our governments have frequently adopted "industrial strategies" to achieve social objectives.[172] * Such approaches have been used in the distant past to build railroads, increase steel production and build food security. They have been used in the recent past to secure necessary medicines in Canada and abroad, to protect cultures and to reduce fossil fuel consumption. They can be used in the near future to prevent cancer and heart disease.

* Canadian economist Albert Breton defined industrial strategy for the former Economic Council of Canada as an attempt to reduce the gap between the actual outputs of manufactured goods and the socially optimal level.

Traditional policy tools to implement industrial strategies include tariffs, quotas, subsidies, licensing, protected oligopolies and monopolies, public ownership, private ownership, profit controls, and bans on foreign ownership. These strategies are used to both increase production (as in the domestic music industry), or decrease production (as in the case of taxis or street vendors). They are used to increase consumption (as in the case of inoculation programs), or decrease consumption (as in the case of energy use).

Canadian history is an epic of this type of intervention, and our geography is an album of its legacy. Institutions like the Trans-Canada Railway, prairie farmers' co-operatives, farm product agencies (like the

Wheat Board), energy monopolies (like Ontario Hydro or Hydro-Québec), the CBC, hospitals, schools, parks and the Canada Council have shaped the Canada we know today. Their stories are told as chapters in our history of nation-building.

Governments continue to use industrial strategies to foster the public good where the market has failed to do so. Current measures include amendments to the *Patent Act* to allow for the production of generic drugs to treat AIDS and other illnesses in the developing world. Such strategies are also being developed to manage new challenges—like the Green Car industrial strategy proposed to help Canada comply with Kyoto obligations.[173]

Policies and approaches successfully applied other sectors could help develop such a strategy for tobacco, with the goal of reducing the gap between the actual production of cigarettes (over 40 billion per year[174]) and the health optimal level (near zero).

Weapons

Because armaments and other products with direct applications to warfare pose serious risks to both domestic and international security, their commercial trade is strictly controlled. Military goods are explicitly exempt from WTO trade agreements,[175] allowing governments full sovereign control over this industry. Gun control laws permit private citizens to purchase only a few forms of weapons with sporting applications, subject to an approval process requiring safety training and background checks. The *Export and Import Permits Act* requires exporters of military goods to obtain a permit, issued only after extensive consultations within the departments of Foreign Affairs and National Defense to determine whether the proposed sale could compromise Canada's strategic interests, international obligations, or human rights values.[176]

Relevance to tobacco control: Arms manufacturers are not free to sell their products however and to whomever they please. Measures to reduce the use of armaments are not subject to international trade agreements. Measures used to control the arms trade show:

- the willingness of societies and their governments to impose strict controls on the sale of consumer goods;
- the legitimacy of founding those measures on the inherently harmful characteristics of those goods;
- the ability to protect those measures from trade agreements.

Greenhouse gas emissions

To reduce the growth in emissions of CO_2 and other gasses that alter the global climate, many countries—including Canada—are committing themselves to the reduction objectives contained in the 1992 Kyoto Protocol. Among the mechanisms under discussion is a system of emissions quotas, requiring the issuance of permits to polluters,[177] which would be reduced over time to achieve the goals of the protocol. Proposals to allocate and reduce the number of these permits have been developed with the goal of providing incentives to industries to work toward specific national emissions targets. Many other incentive programs have been adopted to encourage energy reduction, such as rebates on "Energy Smart" appliances, or for retrofitting homes to make them more energy efficient.[178]

Relevance to tobacco control: Tobacco corporations defend their marketing practices on the grounds that they are intended not to increase the size of the market (the number of tobacco consumers), but merely to capture a larger share of the existing market by attracting customers away from competitors.[179] A quota system in the tobacco market, which required reductions in cigarette sales, could create incentives for tobacco corporations to abide by this claim. Proposed greenhouse gas regimes show:

- the willingness and need of governments to set reduction targets;
- the ability of governments to develop innovative mechanisms to achieve targets.

Alcohol

Alcohol, with its association to a variety of medical and social ills, has long been subject to regulatory control. Alcohol management strategies have spanned a control spectrum from retail licensing for certain product categories (wine and beer, but not spirits), through government retail monopolies, "dry" communities (where commercial sales are prohibited), to complete prohibition). These policies have allowed governments to exercise direct control over the availability of alcohol products, and the circumstances under which they will be sold.

Alcohol supply is now managed in a variety of ways in Canada, but in some provinces the retailing of alcohol is managed through a government monopoly (such as the Liquor Control Board of Ontario).[180] Some provinces experimented with prohibition in the early 20th century, and a small number of communities continue to remain "dry."[181] Although this model for alcohol management is challenged by those who prefer a more liberalized alcohol market,[182] Canadian addiction experts report that "alcohol monopolies represent an effective means of balancing public health concerns against fiscal interests and customer convenience."[183] Government-controlled liquor stores can provide "a workable setting for health-related educational materials and campaigns," primarily because they lack the strict profit maximization mandate of private for-profit corporations.[184] Privatized systems with little regulation and open competition tend toward "an increased number of outlets, longer opening hours and increased consumption."[185]

Empirical research confirms that there is a positive correlation between the number and opening hours of liquor establishments and debilitating health concerns. For example, when in 1969 Finland liberalized their alcohol regulations, over 2,000 new retail beer establishments emerged in addition to a 124% rise in beer drinking and a 46% rise in overall alcohol consumption.[186] Furthermore, between 1968 and 1975 an increase in Finnish per capita alcohol consumption of almost 50% was accompanied by a 157% jump in deaths from liver cirrhosis and other alcohol related problems.[187]

Canadian authority Robin Room reports that alcohol monopolies allow governments to "hold down rates of social, health and casualty problems caused by drinking...to hold down the overall level of alcohol sales and...also particularly affect drinking patterns most closely associated with social and health harm. By keeping private interests out of the retail store level, a government monopoly also changes the contours of the political arena in which alcohol policy is debated."[188]

Relevance to tobacco control: Despite three and a half centuries of experience with tobacco monopolies (the first was established in Venice in 1659), governments have primarily used this market intervention as a way of maximizing profits from the sale of tobacco and other controllable imports, such as salt and coffee.[189] Nonetheless, the alcohol consumption patterns of public and private sector alcohol distribution systems bear some important lessons for the tobacco industry.

Although there is no state monopoly for tobacco in Canada, the manufacturing and wholesaling of tobacco in Canada is characteristic of a monopoly/monopsony because 94% of the market is controlled by only three tobacco corporations. The "big three" use their market strength to ensure they have a direct relationship with retailers and a high level of influence in the retailing of their products in order to increase cigarette sales. This monopoly power could be used for very different purposes of it were a public monopoly.

Restricting access to tobacco products by means of public monopolies on wholesale and/or retail sales, similar to those that exist for alcohol, would allow for more effective enforcement of age requirements and tighter controls on point-of-sale promotion. During a review of tobacco retailing by the Prince Edward Island legislative assembly, a coalition of health groups recently recommended that a liquor-store style retail stores be established to manage the supply of tobacco.[190]

Canadian alcohol policies show:

- the willingness of some governments to closely manage the retail of potentially harmful products;
- the willingness of Canadians to accept a variety of approaches to the retailing of potentially harmful products;
- the importance of being clear about whether the objectives of a government-owned industry are to maximize revenues, to decrease use, or to balance those and other objectives.

Canada's gambling laws were substantially liberalized during the twentieth century. At the beginning of the century, gambling (with the exception of horse racing) was prohibited under the *Criminal Code* (1867). Only modest exemptions to the law were allowed until 1969, when the *Criminal Code* was amended to allow federal and provincial governments the ability to use lotteries to fund worthwhile activities and to grant lottery licenses to authorized charitable groups. A further amendment in 1985 gave provinces exclusive control over gambling (including authority over gaming on First Nations' lands), and also permitted governments to oversee video gaming devices (such as VLTs and slot machines). Currently, ticket lotteries, horse racing and charitable gaming are legal in all Canadian provinces, and casinos and slot machines operate in at least seven provinces. VLTs operate in all provinces except Ontario and British Columbia. Internet gambling is prohibited.[191]

Relevance to tobacco control: In less than forty years, public policy on gambling in Canada was transformed from one of national prohibition to a mosaic of provincial regimes. Unlike those in many other countries, Canadian governments have maintained exclusive authority over gaming. The management of gambling in Canada shows:

- Canada's willingness and ability to maintain a different (and more restrictive) regime than other nations;
- the speed with which dramatic changes in public policy can be made and accepted.

Public utilities and public services

In Canada, as elsewhere, the markets for many goods and services are restricted to selected suppliers. Not infrequently, these are sold exclusively through monopolies, either privately or publicly owned and/or managed.

In some cases, the rationale is economic. This is especially the case for "network industries," such as water, sewer, and electricity, whose large infrastructure requirements pose major barriers to entry and thus contribute to the "market failure" of over-pricing or inadequate quality.[192]

Even in cases such as fire services or auto insurance, competition functions but is considered by some to work counter to vital public interests, and these services are often in public hands.

For other sectors, non-economic reasons are also used to justify public administration. Many core services—policing, education and health care—are managed almost entirely through public institutions. Essential utilities and services have been placed under public management, with a mandate to make these services safe, reliable, fairly priced, and available to everyone.[193] The Canadian health care system, for example, was progressively brought under public administration to ensure not-for-profit decision making, comprehensiveness, universality, portability and accessibility.[194]

This system of government-run monopolies is not without critics, some of whom claim that many public utilities are inefficient and that the private sector is capable of providing comparable services at lower costs. Challenges to maintaining government controls over many essential services—such as hospitals and other health care services, energy supply, roads and schools—are frequent and recurrent. Some jurisdictions have made different choices about the mix of private and public control over essential services (Alberta charter schools and attempts to privatize Ontario's energy grid are recent examples).

Relevance to tobacco control: The management of utilities and essential public services shows:

- the ability and willingness of governments to radically re-structure the provision of certain goods and services;
- the importance placed on not-for-profit management of certain good and services.

Culture

The Canadian government has implemented "national policies and programs that promote Canadian content, foster cultural participation, active citizenship and participation in Canada's civic life, and strengthen connections among Canadians."[195] A variety of policy tools have been applied to the cultural marketplace. These include:

Public ownership

During the 1930s, in response to what were perceived as abuses by private radio stations operating in Canada and the vulnerability of Canadians to American-owned media, Canadians established, through federal government actions, control over public airwaves. The federal government clarified jurisdiction over the electronic media and created both national institutions like the CBC, and federal laws like the *Broadcasting Act*, to ensure Canadian ownership of the media and to "safeguard, enrich and strengthen the cultural, political, social and economic fabric of Canada."[196] Through ownership, the government has also created a public interest presence when there was a need for active agents in the cultural marketplace. Institutional agents include the National Arts Centre, several national museums, the National Film Board and Telefilm.

The government has also established funding programs, which are aimed at increasing the supply of cultural goods and services. These include the Canadian Magazine Fund, the Publications Assistance Program, the Canadian Television Fund, the Museums Assistance Program, the Canada Music Fund, programs of the Canada Council, the Cultural Industries Development Fund, the Canadian Arts and Heritage Sustainability Program, the Canadian Film or Video Production Tax Credit.[197]

Property rights

Canada provides copyright and other intellectual property protection (which is a form of time-limited monopoly power) to influence the supply of cultural goods.

Regulatory power

In addition to institutions and funding, the government also uses its regulatory power to increase the demand for Canadian cultural services and goods. One of the most noticeable of these is the Canadian content requirements for television and radio broadcasting. Other policies and programs used to increase demand are international expositions, support of Team Canada and other trade actions, and the development of a new international cultural treaty, the International Instrument on Cultural Diversity.[198]

Relevance to tobacco control: Canada's cultural regime suggests that:

- a broad range of tools of varying scope can be combined in a comprehensive industrial strategy to increase and decrease production and consumption of a good or service;
- an industrial strategy can be sustained through a wide range of public and private institutions, administrative and regulatory measures and funding.

FIVE

A tobacco industry that helps people quit

As we saw in the previous chapter, for-profit business corporations are not the only game in town. Many of the other forms of business enterprise are not programmed to maximize profits at anyone's expense, but rather are built to achieve social, health, or environmental goals. These other forms provide valuable models for the design of a tobacco manufacturing industry that would reduce consumption, rather than striving to increase it.

Canadians have many options for reforming the tobacco industry and transforming it into a public health ally. Outlined below are three approaches that could be taken to create a public interest tobacco manufacturer that is programmed to reduce tobacco use.

An illustration of the way tobacco would be supplied by any of these three approaches is shown overleaf. In some ways, the supply of cigarettes would continue as it is today: farmers would grow tobacco, a marketing board would sell it to the manufacturers, the manufacturers would distribute it to retail or other outlets and smokers would purchase it. The key differences are that the whole system would be programmed to discourage starting, to encourage quitting and to phase-out tobacco use, and that the current impediments to doing that would be removed.

Public Interest Tobacco Supply

indirect control	direct management and control	complete control	influence over
FARMERS	**RESEARCH AND DEVELOPMENT**	**DISTRIBUTORS/RETAILERS**	**SMOKERS**
• grow leaf tobacco solely under quota (administered by existing or revamped Tobacco Marketing Board)	• find optimal cigarette designs to promote quitting and reduce onset smoking • find new ways to de-market smoking	• dispense cigarettes and other products under licensing or other agreements • support quitting	• able to acquire cigarettes they find acceptable (no demand for illegal source) • able to acquire useful support in quitting
• commercial growing of tobacco is not allowed outside Marketing Board system.	**MANUFACTURING/PURCHASING**	• receive incentives for helping clients quit	
	• manufacture or purchase cigarettes sufficiently acceptable to smokers to reduce incentives for smuggling	• collaborate with public health agencies	
TOBACCO MARKETING BOARD	• manufacture or purchase products which support quitting	• respond to local conditions and opportunities	
• purchase leaf tobacco	• manufacture or purchase products which reduce harm		
• sell leaf tobacco to manufacturer	**MARKETING**		
• manage planned phase-out of tobacco production	• progressively de-brand cigarettes (through communication and reduced brand elements on packages, etc)		
• administer transition program or payments to farmers	• promote quitting • discourage starting		

A different way of selling cigarettes

The new tobacco manufacturer would have a familiar operating structure, but instead of a profit motivation, it would be motivated to reduce smoking.

On the surface, many of its operations would be similar to those we see today. The same employees would still order tobacco from the same growers, other employees would supervise the machinery that converts it into cigarettes and packages them, and other employees would continue to load it onto trucks to market. At a higher level in the corporate hierarchy, supervisors would supervise, and managers would manage.

The key difference is that this work would be done under very different directions from senior management. The new executive and senior management would direct all work towards the tobacco consumption reduction goals.

This would help create a corporate culture of commitment to public health improvement. All employees would become part of an exciting new public health enterprise. Instead of selling more and more cigarettes, the corporation would actually give customers what the vast majority of them want—help with quitting smoking. The Research & Development Department would embrace the new challenge of developing products that are less hazardous and sell less, and the Marketing Department would be challenged to sell health and de-market tobacco.

The new system would also:

- work with public health authorities, researchers, and other organizations in devising and implementing smoking reduction initiatives;
- cease all advertising and promotion aimed at increasing demand;
- commence "de-marketing" campaigns to reduce demand;
- use pricing strategies to balance the need to encourage quitting, encourage continuing addicts to use safer nicotine sources (i.e. patch, chewing pieces), discourage smuggling, address health consequences of regressive impact of any price increases on consumer income;
- adjust cigarette design to encourage quitting and discourage uptake (make cigarettes less addictive, and less attractive);

- Gradually transform the current retail environment to one more appropriate for addiction treatment, and provide incentives and disincentives to accelerate this process (in such a reformed distribution system, retailers would no longer be paid for point-of-sale visual displays or for selling more cigarettes but would be given incentives to encourage quitting by offering cessation assistance and recruiting quitters);
- research ways to reduce smoking (including funding research by others);
- fund implementation of those mechanisms;
- work with government in develop innovative mechanisms to stop contraband tobacco (smuggling and illicit manufacture);
- engage other elements of the public health system (physicians, public health units, addiction treatment centres, etc) in programs and other tobacco reduction initiatives;
- develop new strategies and approaches to accelerate reductions in tobacco use.

What the new system would *not* do is victimize smokers. This is not a proposal to ban possession or consumption of tobacco. The industry has already victimized tobacco users by spreading and fostering addiction. Our proposal, in any of its variations, provides users with the substance they want, while offering assistance in quitting to the vast majority who do want to quit.

There are many forms this new system could take: each of the three models below is intended to illustrate one option. They are not policy prescriptions for what an industry *must* or even *should* look like. Rather they are different illustrations of what they *could* look like.

Model A: Private sector — public interest model

Overview

This model involves the creation of two private-sector non-profit organizations designed to reduce tobacco use. These organizations would together carry out all Canadian manufacture and importing. Growing, wholesaling, and retailing would not be directly modified in this model, but the monopoly power of the manufacturer would result in significant changes to the way cigarettes are sold.

The **Tobacco Manufacturing Association** (TMA or Association) would purchase tobacco, manufacture cigarettes, and sell them to distributors. It would also work to reduce tobacco consumption.

The **Tobacco Consumption Reduction Foundation** (TCRF or Foundation) would receive all revenues of the Association in excess of its costs, and distribute them to various tobacco consumption reduction initiatives, including providing performance incentives to the Association to reduce consumption.

Relationship to government

Both agencies would be operate fully independent of government.

Analogous organizations or systems

The Tobacco Manufacturing Association would be analogous to private sector commercial enterprises that have a social mandate instead of a solely for-profit mandate, such as the Desjardins Group, Ten Thousand Villages, Makivik Corporation and Goodwill Industries.

The Tobacco Consumption Reduction Foundation would be analogous to private sector foundations that receive revenue from various investments and other sources, and distribute them to organizations that pursue a non-profit mission, such as the Ford Foundation and the Vancouver Foundation, etc.

Organizational goals and mission

The legislated purposes of the Association would be:

- to manufacture and sell to retailers all tobacco products sold in the Canadian consumer market;
- to take all steps within its power to reduce tobacco consumption generally, and specifically to meet minimum targets for consumption

reduction set by the legislation, as well as more stringent annual targets set by the TCRF.

The legislated purposes of the Foundation would be:

- to consult with health professionals, smokers, tobacco control organizations, governments and other stakeholders to set a schedule of annual tobacco consumption reduction targets, that over time will exceed the rates of reduction in all other countries in the world;
- to fund research and implementation of consumption reduction strategies;
- to receive, manage, and distribute the surplus revenues of the Agency so as to maximize consumption reductions.

Incentives to reach the goals (carrots and sticks)

The Foundation would provide the Association modest incentive payments in years that the published targets for consumption reduction are met or exceeded. The Association would be required to distribute incentive payments in such as way as to maximize future reductions:

- all directors, managers and employees receive modest remuneration incentive, subject to legislated formula and cap;
- all members receive modest incentive payment, subject to legislated formula and cap.

The Association would make any remaining surplus available to tobacco consumption research and program funding up to a cap equivalent to double the current amount of such funding. Any remaining surplus would be divided among participating governments.

If the Association failed to meet consumption reduction targets in any year, incentives would not be paid. In addition, the Association would be required to develop a plan for corrective action, present it to the Council of Stakeholders prior to its annual meeting and implement the plan as approved at the meeting.

If the Association failed to meet consumption reduction targets in two consecutive years, the entire Board of Directors would be required to retire at the annual meeting and elections held for a new board. A plan for corrective action would also be required.

The founding legislation would also state minimum targets for consumption reduction. If these are not met, Parliament would be able to put in place any mechanisms needed to ensure the targets are met.

Ownership and internal accountability mechanisms

The Association would not be owned by shareholders in the traditional sense of a business corporation (there would be no entitlement to capital gains or dividends). Its members, who would have the power to vote and elect its board of directors at annual meetings, would include bona fide tobacco control organizations and researchers from different areas of tobacco control experience, such as medical research, public education, law/economics, etc. These members would be selected (and could be removed) by a public, transparent process based on selection criteria expressed in the legislation. Such criteria could include no previous association with tobacco industry or tobacco promotion or related corporations or industries, a demonstrable long-term involvement with tobacco control, etc.

Internally, the normal accountability mechanisms would apply. Employees would report to management, management would report to the Board of Directors, the Board of Directors would report to members. Additionally, the Association would be required to report publicly and to the Foundation on its activities, finances, sales and achievement of its non-profit, for health purposes.

As with the Association, the Foundation would be supervised by a Council of Stakeholders, and be required to report publicly.

Regulatory framework and external accountability mechanisms

Legislation would be passed to create and shape the Association and the Foundation, and to give the Association exclusive rights to manufacture and import tobacco products and provide them to retailers or other distributors.

Although both agencies would be independent of government, as with any profit or non-profit undertaking in the private sector:

- the government would receive and monitor corporate reports and filings, and take action when needed;
- the government would monitor activities to ensure legality, and take action when needed.

In light of the public policy function served by both agencies, the government would additionally monitor performance against minimum legislated consumption reduction targets set in legislation, and take action when needed.

Monopoly/oligopoly/competitive environment

The Association would be the sole manufacturer or importer of tobacco products, and the sole body able to provide tobacco products to retailers. It would have the authority to subcontract certain aspects of its operations that had no impact on the achievement of its purposes.

Taxation and government revenues

Governments would continue to receive tobacco tax revenues, as before. The revenues would flow through the Foundation and would be capped at present per-cigarette and per-jurisdiction levels, so as to eliminate any incentive to government to create policy that might increase consumption.

Government tobacco tax revenues would decline more quickly than they are currently predicted to decline, as tobacco consumption declines more quickly. However, government revenues would be bolstered by their share of incentives when consumption reductions are on track. And government expenditures would decline substantially as the Association and Foundation absorb the costs of research and programs and the costs of tobacco litigation (including defending government programs) is ended. Reduced health care costs in the long-term would be substantial, and would likely result in a large net improvement in government financial position.

Impact on tobacco workers

All current employees who work for tobacco corporations and who agree to abide by the mission statement of the new CTC would be guaranteed jobs for the two year period following the purchase of the industry. Tobacco consumption would decline faster than it is declining at present, and thus there would be long-term shrinkages in the workforce. These would be accomplished first through natural attrition, voluntary separations, job-training and job-placement programs.

Where these are not sufficient, layoffs would occur, but at a maximum rate of one-half of the rate that the industry is currently laying off employees due to mechanization.

Model B: Crown corporation model

Overview

This model would involve the creation of two crown agencies designed to pursue the mandate of tobacco consumption reduction. These organizations would together carry out all Canadian manufacture and importing.

The **Canadian Tobacco Supply Agency** (CTSA or Agency) would be responsible for all short-term and long-term operations in managing the supply of and demand for tobacco.

The **Canadian Tobacco Control Board** (CTCB or Board) would manage revenue surpluses and deficits and ensures the proper operation of the incentive schemes to discourage consumption. The CTCB ensures that the objectives of the Agency are properly set and adjusted in a manner that would ensure that its legislated mandate is being met or exceeded.

Relationship to government

Both Crown corporations would operate at arm's length from government and at arm's length from each other.

Analogous organizations or systems

The Canadian Tobacco Supply Agency and the Canadian Tobacco Control Board would relate to each other in much the same way that the United Way relates to the agencies for which its raises money, or the way a city-wide Health Trust relates to all the hospitals and other health care agencies in the city.

Another analogous structural relationship is that between Atomic Energy Canada Limited and the Atomic Energy Control Board.

Organizational goals and mission

The legislated purposes of the Agency would be to:

- achieve near zero tobacco consumption by the year 2030 through measures designed to discourage demand and limit supply;
- do all that is reasonably possible to prevent the uptake of tobacco use by never-smokers and relapse to smoking by former smokers;
- discourage smoking among current smokers and provide assistance to them for smoking cessation;
- assure that existing demand for tobacco products is satisfied;
- minimize all supplies of contraband tobacco.

The Board would be responsible for ensuring that the objectives of the Agency are properly set and adjusted in a manner that would ensure that its legislated mandate is being met or exceeded. Annual sales targets can be adjusted periodically, possibly as frequently as once a year, but the goal will remain of near-zero consumption by 2030.

An example of the targets the Board could use would be a decline in tobacco consumption of 2 billion cigarettes per year until 2017 and 1 billion per year from 2018 to 2030, by which time consumption would have dropped to near-zero (300 million cigarettes). Another example would be targets to reduce the proportion of Canadians who smoked.

Incentives to reach the goals (carrots and sticks)

The Agency would operate under an incentive structure that provides financial rewards for meeting sales reduction targets and larger rewards for exceeding reduction targets. Rewards would be withheld when targets are not met.

The Agency would collect and manage revenues from sales up to its annual targets. Should sales exceed annual targets, revenues flow immediately to the Canadian Tobacco Control Board. When annual sales targets are met, the Board pays performance bonuses to the Agency. Should sales be even lower than targets, the size of the bonuses increases. The Agency can then spend its bonuses on a number of approved activities, which could include:

- personal salary bonuses for employees;
- pension and severance payments, with payouts to suppliers and distributors as there is less and less need for their services;
- assistance in the development of alternate health-promoting lines of products and services as new lines for existing suppliers and distributors;
- social marketing (public health, social services, environmental protection, etc.);
- charitable donations;
- strengthening tobacco control in developing countries;
- helping to phase out tobacco in the other 191 member states of the WHO.

Ownership and internal accountability mechanisms

Both organizations would be Crown corporations and thus owned by government.

The Agency and Board would each have their own Board of Directors with representation from federal, provincial and territorial governments, public health agencies, business and each other. Both agencies would be accountable to their Boards of Directors and the Boards of Directors would be accountable to Parliament.

The Board would serve as watchdog agency on the operations of the Agency and would be responsible for monitoring and oversight of achievement of tobacco reduction targets on schedule. Any requested adjustments to the schedule would have to be approved by the Board.

Regulatory framework and external accountability mechanisms

A new Act of Parliament (ideally agreed to by the provinces and territories), would authorize the purchase of all existing tobacco corporations and their being merged into the new Canadian Tobacco Supply Agency.

The Act would create the Agency and the Board and outline the broad parameters of their structure and function.

Both agencies would be governed by the *Financial Administration Act* and subject to audit by the Auditor General.

Monopoly/oligopoly/competitive environment

The Agency would be the sole manufacturer and importer of tobacco and tobacco products.

Taxation and government revenues

The government would continue to collect tobacco taxes, as before. However, the government should begin planning now for lower tobacco tax revenues in 20-30 years. Government anti-tobacco programs would remain in place (Health Canada and other departments). Close collaboration between government and the Agency would be encouraged in discouraging tobacco supply and demand.

The Board acts as a financial go-between between the Agency and the government. When excess cash is generated over and above needed reserves, the Trust Fund would pay the excess to the government. The Trust Fund would have its revenues topped up by government when revenues fall short of the need for legislatively mandated incentives.

Impact on tobacco workers

All current employees who work for tobacco corporations and who agree to abide by the mission statement of the new Agency would be guaranteed jobs for the two year period following the purchase of the industry. Tobacco consumption would decline faster than it is declining at present, and thus there would be long-term shrinkages in the workforce. These would be accomplished first through natural attrition, voluntary separations, job-training and job-placement programs.

As tobacco use is reduced, the workforce and capacity of the Agency, if directed by Parliament, could be redeployed to address other health challenges, thus usefully applying the knowledge gained in reducing smoking.

Model C: Licensing commission model

Overview

The **Tobacco Control Commission** (TCC or Commission) would be an arms' length federal government agency with regulatory authority over the entire system of tobacco supply.

In exercising that authority, it would apply direct controls over those parts of the supply chain it felt required strict oversight (likely the design and manufacture of cigarettes) and indirect controls over the parts of the supply chain it felt were best managed in partnership with other (non-profit) agencies, other federal government agencies, or other levels of government.

The TCC would be a single independent public authority over a single system of tobacco supply, but would engage multiple health partners in its work. This system would include a public regulatory agency and private and public sector partners all working in the public interest.

Relationship to government

This government agency would operate at arm's length from government, but report to Parliament.

Analogous organizations or systems

The Tobacco Control Commission is analogous to the Canadian Radio-Television and Telecommunications Commission (CRTC) in that it has authority over a single system, but engages multiple partners. Unlike the CRTC, which oversees a mixed private/profit sector of broadcasters and communications providers, the TCC would ensure that the tobacco system was managed on a non-profit basis only.

It is also analogous to other "systems" approaches, such as those used to manage infectious disease control or other cross-jurisdictional health management.

Organizational goals and mission

The legislated purposes of the Commission would be to:

- control the supply of all tobacco products to the Canadian market through regulatory and administrative arrangements;
- achieve specified benchmarks in the reduction of prevalence.

An example of a set of benchmarks that could be used would be a reduction in prevalence to 15% within five years, 10% within 10 years and 5% within 15 years. Decreases in per-capita consumption of cigarettes are another benchmark approach that could be used.

The founding legislation would require Parliament to review the agency's mandate at the end of 15 years.

Incentives to reach the goals (carrots and sticks)

The Commission would have the administrative flexibility and regulatory authority to develop and employ incentives it deems suitable to obtain results from various components of the supply chain.

If the agency failed to achieve a benchmark by more than one percentage point (for example, if it failed to reduce smoking to at least 16% within five years using the benchmarks identified above), the Governor in Council would be compelled to establish an independent judicial inquiry to recommend remedial action.

Ownership and internal accountability mechanisms

The Commission would be owned by the federal government. It could, like the Canada Pension Plan Investment Board, involve each provincial government on a board of stewards.

Commissioners on the TCC would be government appointees, but their appointment would be subject to review by Parliament.

Eligibility for appointment to the Commission would be restricted to those with demonstrated health expertise. Salaries, benefits and other incentives for the employees would be consistent with those of other crown agencies.

Regulatory framework and external accountability mechanisms

The Commission would be established by an Act of Parliament, ideally with the agreement of the provinces. It would have a similar level of independence and same reporting relationship to Parliament as the Canada Pension Plan Investment Board, the Canadian Broadcasting Corporation or the Bank of Canada currently have.

Provincial Ministries of Health would be consulted before appointments to the commission were made and would be given the opportunity to recommend individuals for appointment.

Monopoly/oligopoly/competitive environment

The Commission would determine whether monopoly, oligopoly or competition is desirable at each link in the tobacco supply chain.

By way of illustration, the Commission could enter into an exclusive arrangement for tobacco supply with Canada Post in some provinces (monopoly distribution), but make arrangements with community health centres and public health units (oligopoly) in other regions while, at the same time, use incentives for community groups to compete for success with quit centres (competition).

Taxation and government revenues

Upon creation of the Commission, provincial and federal governments would no longer collect tobacco taxes, and all revenues from cigarette sales would flow to the TCC.

Governments would consequently benefit from tobacco sales, but they would no longer have direct control over cigarette prices and would consequently no longer be perceived to be in a conflict of interest over tobacco tax revenues.

Surplus revenues would be returned to the consolidated revenue fund. The budget for the TCC would require parliamentary approval, but it would finance all its operations from tobacco sales until prevalence had fallen below 5% (within 15 years).

Impact on tobacco workers

Employees who currently work for tobacco corporations and who agree to abide by the mission statement of the Commission would be provided employment, and their expertise would be applied towards the task of "demarketing" tobacco.

Because tobacco consumption would decline faster than it is declining at present, there would inevitably be long-term shrinkages in the

Private vs. Public Interests and Sectors
Choices for Tobacco Suppliers

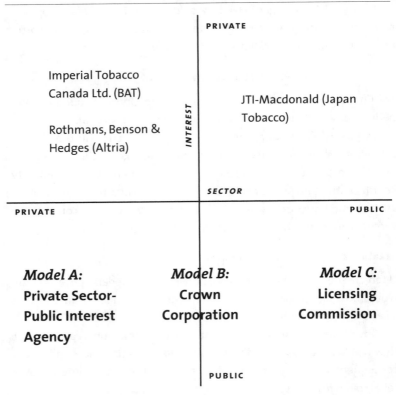

workforce. These would be accomplished first through natural attrition, voluntary separations, job-training and job-placement programs.

A range of *public interest* options

The three models proposed above would all ensure that tobacco is managed in the public interest, but are not all public sector models. As the figure above illustrates, they span the range of private sector to mixed public-private sector to public sector. When compared with the existing

Relationship of Governments to the
Public-Interest Tobacco Monopoly

PARLIAMENT OF CANADA

- passes legislation creating new system
- reviews and approves annual budget (Models B, C)
- reviews performance of agency (Model A)
- recommends actions
- enacts changes when needed

FEDERAL AND PROVINCIAL MINISTERS OF REVENUE

- acquires tobacco corporations and transfers assets to new system
- receives payments to cover cost of purchase either through taxes (Model A, B) or payments (model C)
- receives excess revenues from system during tobacco phase out
- replaces tobacco taxes with other revenue sources

FEDERAL AND PROVINCIAL MINISTERS OF HEALTH

- monitors progress
- recommends (and regulates) actions
- engages formally and informally in smoking-reduction actions

GOVERNOR IN COUNCIL

- approves legislation creating new system
- monitors activities
- appoints members to the governing boards (Model B, C)
- establishes judicial review if agency fails to meet targets (Model C)

MINISTRIES OF FOREIGN AFFAIRS/TRADE/ DEVELOPMENT

- defends system against trade challenge
- promotes Canadian expertise in tobacco reduction overseas
- supports tobacco reduction efforts in other countries

LAW ENFORCEMENT

- monitors illegal manufacture, imports or sales of cigarettes
- recommend actions
- engages formally and informally as appropriate and/or needed

PUBLIC INTEREST TOBACCO SUPPLY

Relationship of Civil Society to the
Public-Interest Tobacco Monopoly

**PUBLIC INTEREST
TOBACCO SUPPLY**

RESEARCH COMMUNITY

- collaborate formally and informally with the agency
- conduct research on behalf of the agency
- conduct independent research on tobacco use

NON GOVERNMENTAL ORGANIZATIONS

- engage formally and informally with the agency
- manage cessation projects or distribution of tobacco/nicotine products under agreement to the agency, as appropriate or desired
- recommend actions to the agency
- independently monitor and report on progress of agency

LOCAL PUBLIC HEALTH UNITS

- engage formally and informally with the agency
- recommend actions to government regarding agency
- recommend actions to the agency
- manage projects which help smokers quit and prevent up-take of smoking
- distribute tobacco/nicotine products as appropriate or desired

three big tobacco companies, we see a fuller range of ways to manage tobacco than are currently in place. These include:

- Private sector serving public interest: Model A (a private non-profit tobacco manufacturer);
- Mixed private/public sector but serving public interest: Model C (a government Licensing Commission);
- Public sector serving public interest: Model B (a Crown corporation);
- Private sector serving private interest: the current role of Imperial Tobacco Canada Ltd and Rothmans, Benson & Hedges Ltd.;
- Public sector serving private interest: JTI-Macdonald is wholly owned by Japan Tobacco, in which the government of Japan is the largest and controlling shareholder. Japan Tobacco is thus at least partially owned by the public sector, but sells cigarettes in Canada and other

countries (including Japan) in ways undistinguishable from privately owned tobacco companies (like BAT and Altria).

Relationship with government

In many aspects, the relationship between a tobacco industry modeled after any of these proposals would share the same structure as that currently in place. The industry would operate under legislated authority (only in this case, separate legislation would apply, and not federal or provincial corporate law), Health Ministries would continue to set health regulations, law enforcement would continue to protect against smuggling and other illegal sales.

In other profound ways, the relationship would be entirely different. Governments and the reformed tobacco industry would be working towards the same goal—a goal that is democratically developed and clarified in legislation

Relationship with civil society

Significant changes could be expected in the relationship between a transformed tobacco industry and those engaged "on the ground" to reduce tobacco use. Today, these sectors work against each other's interests, and are mandated to do so by their charters. Public health organizations, like the Cancer Society, the Heart and Stroke Foundation, the Lung Association and local health authorities are mandated to protect health (and subsequently to reduce smoking). Tobacco corporations are mandated to increase profits (and subsequently to increase smoking)

In a system where the suppliers of tobacco and health organizations share the mandate to promote health by reducing smoking, these communities would, for the first time, work in common cause. Physicians and retailers would no longer be divided by the issue of tobacco, but would be united by the challenge of meeting tobacco reduction quotas, and managing the resulting workplace or agricultural transitions in ways that protect the health and dignity of all Canadians.

The long-term future for the new system

In the longer term, as tobacco consumption in Canada reaches near-zero levels, vastly lower levels of production would be required. However, it would remain important not to allow foreign tobacco corporations to begin marketing to future generations of Canadians. Thus the public-interest tobacco system would continue to be the sole provider of tobacco products in Canada, and would continue its mandate of reducing tobacco consumption.

It would also assist in the phasing out of tobacco in other countries. There are 191 other member states of the World Health Organization that could all benefit from Canadian success and expertise in phasing out tobacco in their countries. If and when the rest of the world catches up in managing the tobacco epidemic, and the global trade in tobacco is completely eliminated, plans can be made for permanent bans on tobacco production and sales, and the orderly wind-up of the tobacco supply function. Along the way, new opportunities would be created for new lines of work borne of the experience of the planned phase-out of tobacco in Canada (e.g. social marketing of other healthy or socially-worthwhile products and services, such as healthy eating, fitness, environmental protection, social housing, mass transit, etc.).

The right—and the capacity—to make this change.

When considering replacing the old for-profit, consumption-boosting tobacco industry with a new for-health, consumption-reducing tobacco industry, questions that might arise in the minds of some people are "Can this be done?" "Can we afford it?" "What about trade regimes?" "Goes government even have the legal authority?" The short answer to each of these questions is yes.

The only legal constraint on the authority of Parliament or a provincial legislature is the Constitution. There is nothing in the Constitution that gives tobacco corporations immunity from being purchased and transformed, and government is entitled to restrict and control sales of tobacco or any harmful substance to those authorized in statute.

The legislation enabling the industry transformation would prohibit the manufacture of tobacco products with one exemption—the public interest manufacturer. The legislation, in order to cover imports, would also prohibit the sale of tobacco products, with an exemption for the public interest manufacturer and anyone to whom the public interest manufacturer had sold the products. In this manner, all tobacco products—made domestically or abroad—would flow through the public interest manufacturer. The legislation would also allow for the government to purchase shares in existing tobacco corporations, and to transfer ownership of plants and other facilities to the public interest manufacturer.

Division of powers

Only the Supreme Court of Canada can definitively rule whether a law restricting the manufacture and sale of cigarettes is within the legislative competence of the federal Parliament as opposed to that of the provincial legislatures. High courts across the country and the Supreme Court of Canada have recognized the extensive powers of both senior levels of government to control many aspects of tobacco industry.[199] The federal Parliament has the criminal law powers and the peace, order and good government powers, both broad and successfully tested in courts on previous tobacco laws. The Supreme Court of Canada has specifically stated in respect of the federal criminal law power:

> [I]t is clear that Parliament could, if it chose, validly prohibit the manufacture and sale of tobacco products under the criminal law power on the ground that these products constitute a danger to public health. Such a prohibition would be directly analogous to the prohibitions on dangerous drugs and unsanitary foods or poisons

mentioned earlier, which quite clearly fall within the federal crimi-
nal law power. [200]

The provincial legislatures also have the ability to legislate in respect of health. And the property and civil rights power and the power to regulate in respect of local issues both give provincial legislatures a broad jurisdiction to regulate industries in a number of ways.

It may be prudent to reach federal-provincial agreements to pass compatible legislation at both levels to transform the industry. Areas of overlapping jurisdiction are quite common in Canada: food safety; pesticides; transportation of dangerous goods; toxins etc. The Supreme Court of Canada confirmed in a recent ruling against the tobacco industry that provincial legislation is valid even if a federal law in the same area has different rules and standards. As long as it is possible to comply with both laws and the provincial law doesn't undermine the intent of the federal law, both can validly restrict activities even to differing levels. [201]

It is unlikely that parallel provincial legislation is required, but getting clear provincial support through parallel provincial laws could reduce the duration and cost of any court challenge mounted by the industry. Provinces that choose to join in the new system could be eligible for financial incentives when their local rate of tobacco consumption declines, and would be exempt from the rules governing imports and exports to foreign jurisdictions. Their populations would be come healthier more quickly, and their governments would avoid the policy interference of the for-profit industry.

The Charter

Similarly, only the Supreme Court of Canada can definitively rule on whether a particular law violates the Charter rights of a person or corporation. It is clear that a tobacco corporation cannot claim that the Charter protects its "right to life" under section 7: "a corporation cannot avail itself of the protection offered by s. 7 of the Charter." [202] Nor can it claim that its "freedom of association" under section 2(d) of the charter would be violated by prohibiting its dealing in tobacco. [203] Only the ability to associate is protected by s.2(d), not the ability to undertake the activities of the association.

A tobacco corporation may attempt to use other sections of the Charter, but in our view it is very unlikely that it would succeed in doing so. And if it did, it would be unlikely to succeed in a Charter section 1 analysis of whether such a violation were a justified infringement.[*]

Thus, although only the Supreme Court can decide in the end, it is unlikely that a tobacco corporation would succeed in constitutionally challenging legislation that converted the tobacco industry from a profit maximizing industry that increases smoking into a health maximizing industry that reduces smoking. Canada abounds with examples of restrictions on the sale of various substances, licensing systems, and public sector enterprises; they are a clear part of our government's mandate to protect its citizens. Of course, this is not to say that the tobacco corporations won't **try** to challenge the new legislation.

The final tobacco court challenge

Whatever legislation is passed to transform the tobacco industry into a consumption-reducing, health promoting industry, it would likely be challenged by the industry in court. The tobacco industry has a long history of challenging health-promotion legislation, and would likely do so in this case.

However, the factors motivating such a challenge would be slightly different this time. In their previous litigation challenging public health measures like advertising restrictions, tobacco corporations have been serving the interests of their shareholders. Advertising sells more cigarettes and thus keeps profits and share values up. In this case, the motives may different. Tobacco corporation directors and executives would likely initiate lobbying and court challenges again. After all, some of them may lose their positions and part of their (substantial) incomes when the reform comes. They would no doubt tell shareholders (not to mention taxpayers, smokers, employees, tobacco growers and anyone else who would listen) that this change is bad for them and that it needs to be challenged in court — using shareholder money.

However, this time a legal challenge might not be in the interests of shareholders. There are many scenarios under which **it could be clearly in the shareholder's interest to take a certain payment over an uncertain future.** Such scenarios include one where the pot is sweetened with

[*] Even if a court upheld a tobacco corporation charter claim, the government could invoke the 'notwithstanding' clause to ensure its authority to make this change. The barriers to doing this are political, not constitutional.

a premium payment for quick sale, or one where litigation against the companies makes their future value highly uncertain. Under these conditions, the best thing for the shareholders' investments would be for the corporations and their directors and executives to cooperate in the arrangement, save the legal bills, and allow the shareholders to pocket the proceeds and invest elsewhere. Fighting against a proposal to give shareholders the best anticipated value would not be in the interests of the shareholders.

One thing is very clear. When the tobacco industry does get transformed, once the legal challenges had been put to bed there would be *no future challenges of public health measures by tobacco corporations*. This alone would save a lot of money on legal bills—money that taxpayers seem to be paying all the time now.

There may be a constitutional challenge to the legislation bringing in this change, but it won't succeed. It would be the last such challenge; public health measures put in place after the transformation of the industry would be supported by, rather than litigated against, by a public-interest tobacco manufacturer.

The right under international agreements

International trade agreements

Canada has made a number of international undertakings that affect the ability of governments to make domestic or international policy.[204]

Some of these undertakings are in the form of multilateral trade agreements, such as the North American Free Trade Agreement (NAFTA) or the World Trade Organization agreements (WTO), others are bilateral agreements, like those entered into with Chile and Israel.

The wide range of these commercial agreements, and the global nature of the tobacco business creates a climate where it is easy for tobacco companies (if they can lobby governments to support their case) to use trade threats in vexatious ways.* Preparing for a trade challenge would be due diligence in the development of a public-interest tobacco manufacturer.

* Philip Morris, for example, responded to Canada's proposals to use generic packaging of cigarettes and to ban the use of the misleading descriptor 'light' by saying these measures would infringe the NAFTA and TRIPS agreements.

The set of WTO agreements that could be used by multinational tobacco companies to threaten a decision to bring tobacco under the control of public interest organizations (whether they are government or
private non-profit organizations) include the **Multilateral Agreements on
Trade in Goods** (which include 12 specific agreements, including those on
Agriculture, Sanitary and Phytosanitary Measures, Textiles and Clothing,
Technical Barriers to Trade, Trade-Related Investment Measures, etc.),
the **General Agreement on Trade in Services (GATS)** and the **Agreement
on Trade-Related Aspects of Intellectual Property Rights (TRIPS)**.

These and other commercial agreements have different provisions
and dispute settlement mechanisms, but share some common obligations, including:

- **national treatment,** or the obligation of countries to treat imported
  foreign goods equally to those produced domestically, and to treat
  foreign trading partners equally to domestic producers;
- **most favoured-nation treatment,** or the requirement that any trade
  advantage (such as tariff reductions) that is provided to one trading partner must be provided to all trading partners (this principle is
  found in the first article of the GATT);
- **the prohibition on "quantitative restrictions,"** meaning that countries cannot use quotas to restrict imports or exports of products;
- the obligation to treat **"like products"** from other countries equally
  to domestic products;
- the requirement to use the **least trade-restrictive means** of achieving
  its policy goals;
- the **"necessity" test** by which countries must prove that the challenged measures are both needed and are supported by evidence.

Establishing a regime which restricts imports and establishes a monopoly manufacturer might be considered to infringe the principles of
national treatment (because imports would be restricted), "like products" (because foreign branded cigarettes would have to meet onerous
Canadian requirements considered to be tantamount to an import ban),
"quantitative restrictions" (because cigarette supply would be gradually
decreased through supply controls) and "least trade restrictive" (if it is
argued that the same effect could be managed without impacting in-

ternational commerce). The lack of evidence about the difference such a regime could make may hinder the ability to demonstrate "necessity."

There may also be concerns that such a public-interest Canadian tobacco enterprise would breach specific elements of trade agreements, including the investment protection measures of NAFTA (for which a U.S. based company could launch an investor-state complaint). NAFTA guarantees that investors would be compensated for expropriation, but each model of our proposal includes fair compensation. Other arguments might be raised with respect to the Technical Barriers to Trade Agreement, or it may be claimed there is the deviation from international standards preferred by the Sanitary and Phytosanitary Agreement, or the use of trademarks, as protected by the Agreement on Trade-Related Aspects of Intellectual Property Rights (TRIPS).

Trade regimes generally prohibit restrictions on imports[205] and require countries to treat foreign providers of goods and services at least as well as they would treat domestic providers.[206] In the present case, import controls would be needed in order to prevent the domestic public-interest system from being undermined. In theory, restricting altogether the imports of tobacco products could offend these trade regimes. However a GATT panel has already confirmed that under GATT a government can establish a

> monopoly to regulate the overall supply of cigarettes, their prices and their retail availability provided it thereby does not accord imported cigarettes less favourable treatment than domestic cigarettes.[207]

Provisions in NAFTA confirm that it too does not prohibit Canada (or the US or Mexico) from establishing monopolies, state enterprises, or government-owned monopolies.[208] Canada's public interest tobacco manufacturer would fit this role—being a monopoly that regulated manufacture, supply, prices and retail availability. The measures would be adopted in a transparent way for health purposes, not for nationalist economic purposes.

Important context to a potential trade challenge to Canada's decision to bring tobacco under public interest control is the size of a potential award against Canada. Canadian smokers do not buy foreign-made cigarettes (imported cigarettes make up less than 1% of the Canadian tobacco market).[209] It would be very difficult for a foreign government to demonstrate to a trade tribunal that any restrictions caused by the purchasing practices of a monopoly were tantamount to a ban on imports when, under a centuries-old free market, imports had failed to capture market share. Moreover, the models we propose are clearly aimed at phasing out tobacco use (and this aim is part of the legislation). "Future revenues" that would be foregone would be very small.

Countries which lose a trade challenge are not obliged to change their policies accordingly, although they do have to accept the economic penalties, usually in the form of retaliatory tariffs, for doing so. (The European Union, by way of illustration, lost a challenge against its ban on the import of hormone-treated beef but has decided not to rescind the ban.[210]) Even in the worst-case scenario where a trade panel decided that a Canadian public interest monopoly was unjustified barrier to trade, Canada would have the option to accept a penalty equal to the foregone revenue of imports, which, as we saw above, would not be very high.

A full trade analysis is beyond the scope of this review. The potential for trade challenge is real, and not to be lightly dismissed. But equally real (and not to be lightly dismissed) is the entitlement of countries, within the international trade regime, to take measures to protect the health of their citizens. As the Declaration ending the Fourth WTO Ministerial Conference in 2001 put it:

> We recognize that under WTO rules no country should be prevented from taking measures for the protection of human, animal or plant life or health, or of the environment at the levels it considers appropriate, subject to the requirement that they are not applied in a manner which would constitute a means of arbitrary or unjustifiable discrimination between countries where the same conditions prevail, or a disguised restriction on international trade, and are otherwise in accordance with the provisions of the WTO Agreements.[211]

Trade regimes are only one set of international rules to which Canada has agreed to adhere. Other treaties require that Canada implement effective tobacco control measures, and that she protect the health of her citizens.

The Framework Convention on Tobacco Control

Among the international undertakings Canada has made are a number relating to health. One of the most recent of these is the new global tobacco treaty, the Framework Convention on Tobacco Control. On November 26, 2004, Canada ratified this treaty and on February 27, 2005 this world's first modern public health treaty came into effect.

The FCTC includes several specific obligations (like warning labels that cover at least 30% of the cigarette package, bans on misleading labelling) and general obligations (like implementing public education programs). The objectives and guiding principles of this global health innovation are a clear articulation of the importance that governments give to global collaboration on tobacco control and to the breadth of measures that are needed to "continually and substantially" reduce smoking.

Proposals to acquire and reprogram tobacco companies to reduce smoking are entirely consistent with all FCTC obligations. They provide government with an even broader scope of authority over the administrative, legislative, regulatory and executive measures that the FCTC both encourages and obliges countries to take.

Other international undertakings

* The World Health Organization's constitution defines health as "a state of complete physical, mental and social well-being and not merely the absence of disease or infirmity."

Health obligations are also included in a number of other treaties, including human rights conventions. The "right to health" is recognized explicitly or implicitly in a number of conventions (i.e. the *Universal Declaration of Human Rights*, the *International Covenant on Economic, Social and Cultural Rights*, and the *Convention on the Rights of the Child*).*

A recent report of the United Nations High Commissioner for Refugees (UNHCR) Human Rights' Committee on Economic, Social and Cultural Rights[213] said governments violated that right when they failed to protect them from practices detrimental to health, including "marketing and consumption of tobacco."

Trade vs. Health

The obligations that Canada has undertaken through the Framework Convention on Tobacco Control, and the International Covenant on Economic, Social and Cultural Rights are no less than those entered into under the World Trade Organization commercial treaties. Both sets of agreements give Canada commercial and health rights and both impose commercial and health obligations. Under international law, neither treaty is subordinate to the other (although the convention is to give more recent treaty, in this case the FCTC, precedence).

The FCTC is neither subordinate to, nor supreme over, international trade agreements. It does suggest that the FCTC and other international treaties can be coherent and mutually supporting. The very first line of the FCTC speaks to the importance countries gave to health:

> *Preamble*
> *The Parties to this Convention,*
> **Determined** *to give priority to their right to protect public health*

Article 2 explicitly reinforces the coherence between tobacco control regimes and other (commercial) obligations:

> *Article 2*
> *Relationship between this Convention and other agreements and legal instruments*
> *1. In order to better protect human health, Parties are encouraged to implement measures beyond those required by this Convention and its protocols, and nothing in these instruments shall prevent a Party from imposing stricter requirements that are consistent with their provisions and are in accordance with international law.*

Canada thus has obligations to protect the right of its citizens to health and to do so in ways which are not arbitrary or disguised restrictions on trade. We believe that the approach we propose does both.

Tobacco companies may appeal to international laws (like NAFTA, which allows them to directly challenge governments) and may lobby to get friendly governments to intervene in trade tribunals on their behalf. They would seek to use international law as they use domestic law to defeat, weaken and delay measures that would reduce tobacco sales. International justice, like domestic justice, should not let them succeed.

Financing the purchase

Underlying each of the proposed models for a new style tobacco supplier is the assumption that the government would acquire the existing operation through a purchase agreement. Such an acquisition could be done voluntarily by presenting the owners/shareholders of the current operations an offer they don't want to refuse. The government also has the power and authority to impose a purchase agreement.

The purchase cost of the industry could be financed by normal commercial debt borrowed at the government's borrowing rate, which is lower than the private sector can obtain. The debt could be repaid over a period of one to ten years by ordinary health program spending.

The price of transferring tobacco enterprises from private-interest to public-interest hands, and the negotiations that would establish it, are difficult to predict. Some guidance can be taken private sector acquisitions in the past decade. In 1999, there were significant transfers of ownership of all three transnational tobacco corporations operating in Canada. Full ownership of Imperial Tobacco Canada Ltd was acquired BAT, RJR-Macdonald was sold by RJ Reynolds to Japan Tobacco, and 42% of Rothmans, Benson & Hedges was sold from Rothmans to BAT and then to other shareholders (under an agreement with Canada's Competition Bureau).[214]

During BAT's sale of Rothmans shares, the value of one percent of the Canadian tobacco market was set at $34 million dollars.[215, 216] At that rate, the total value of the market would be $3.4 billion dollars. BAT's purchase of Imperial Tobacco set the price for one percent of the Canadian tobacco market at $153 million.[217] At that rate, the total value of the Canadian market would be $15 billion dollars.

Price in 2005: $0?

In late summer 2004, the Quebec government presented JTI-Macdonald with a bill for $1.36 billion dollars representing the tax revenues lost as a result of the company's involvement in cigarette smuggling. JTI-Macdonald promptly filed for bankruptcy protection.

Legal actions against the corporations are growing. In 2005, the first tobacco-related class action suits were certified (two in Quebec and one in British Columbia). One province, British Columbia, has filed a suit seeking to recover the costs of treating past and future tobacco caused disease. The federal government is also pursuing recovery for taxes lost as a result of industry-organized smuggling.[218] The RCMP has investigated each of the companies for their role in smuggling, and charges have been laid against four companies associated with JTI-Macdonald.[219] These actions may significantly alter the value of the companies and may increase the willingness of some shareholders to sell at a good price.

The government also has the authority to forcibly acquire properties. This sometimes happens when property-owners are reluctant to relinquish their land for the development of a road, a railway, a nature preserve or some other undertaking in the public interest. In such cases, governments provide fair compensation for the value of these properties (NAFTA guarantees this right to investors). Fair compensation would likely also include an evaluation of the financial risks to the industry because of legal action launched (and yet to be launched) by governments seeking compensation for fraudulent tax evasion and health care costs, and others launched (and yet to be launched) by individuals seeking compensation for harm caused by the industry.

A portion of the purchase cost debt could be repaid by future revenues from the sale of tobacco products. Since the consumption of tobacco would decline more rapidly than it currently is declining, future streams of revenue would probably be lower than they are currently projected by the industry. However, costs would be lower than they are for existing tobacco corporations in certain areas. For instance, there would be no more need for tobacco litigation or lobbying, nor for the hundreds of millions of dollars per year that the industry currently spends on marketing and promotion. These and other savings would balance out—perhaps completely—the reduced revenues.

In addition to government expenditures and future revenue streams, the conversion of the industry from for-profit to for-health could attract social investment. Charitable foundations have partnered with government — and have provided funding — to protect the environment in Canada. There is also a possibility of allowing for equity financing along the lines of the Community Interest Company described in Chapter 3. Some of the ethical investing mutual funds in Canada and elsewhere may also invest in this initiative. Having a variety of stakeholders would increase independent scrutiny of the enterprise, not to mention determination by more sectors to make it work.

Purchase of the tobacco corporations by the government would be a sound financial undertaking for government. Firstly, the investment in health would pay off in greatly reduced health care costs from tobacco-induced illness. Second, the profits from the industry, once they paid off the debt, could contribute significantly to government coffers. A formula set in the legislation could divide these revenues between the federal government and participating provincial governments in proportion to the success each province has in reducing its tobacco consumption rate.

The cost of inaction is even higher

If buying tobacco companies seems expensive, the cost of allowing them to continue to serve private-interests is no less costly.

The cost to the Canadian economy of smoking, estimated for 1991 was $15 billion,[220] (a more recent estimate would likely be higher). One in five Canadian deaths is a result of smoking (as are one third of all Canadian cancers).[221] The human and financial cost of leaving business corporations in charge of supplying cigarettes is far greater than the cost of removing them.

Smokers pay dearly — but get little in return

Every year, Canadian smokers open their wallets to purchase cigarettes and provide federal and provincial governments with $8 billion in taxes.* For every dollar paid in tobacco taxes, less than three cents is returned by governments into programs aimed at helping smokers quit, finding ways of reducing the harms of smoking, protecting young people from tobacco marketing or protecting Canadians from second-hand smoke.[222]

* Tobacco tax revenues for provincial and federal governments in 200-2004 were as follows (in millions): Newfoundland, $92.5, Prince Edward Island, $26; Nova Scotia, $162; New Brunswick, $101.3; Quebec, $923; Ontario, $1,350; Manitoba, $190.4; Saskatchewan, $176.7; Alberta, $670; British Columbia, $647; Federal government, $3,350.

Tobacco taxes could be made available to finance the acquisition of tobacco companies in order to improve smoker's health. It would take very little time for the entire costs of the acquisition to be recouped from these funds (an acquisition cost of even $15 billion would require less than two years' tobacco tax revenues).

The full impact on social justice, government finance and public policy dimensions of a temporary diversion of tobacco taxes from general revenues into a program that benefits the taxpayers involved are considerable, and well beyond the scope of this initial review. How willing are governments to forego tobacco taxes? How willing are they to direct taxes into a program to prevent disease instead of treating it? Would this proposal—considering all the health, productivity, litigation, exported profits, advertising and other costs—be more expensive or cheaper to the Canadian economy than the status quo? These and other questions merit public consultation and further study. We simply note that the financial costs would be manageable.

Litigation and other risks

Significant in any discussion of tobacco industry finance is the financial risk from current and potential future litigation. The member/shareholders, directors and managers in the new organizations would need to be legislatively protected from lawsuits for the past wrongs of the for-profit tobacco industry. This protection would not extend to past directors and managers of course, nor to parent corporations.

In compensation for removing some of the potential sources of compensation for tobacco victims, a Tobacco Victims Assistance Fund (TVAF) could be established to provide assistance to the victims of past industry wrongs. The cost of funding and administering the TVAF would be covered by the increase in net present value of the public interest manufacturer when this portion of its costs of future litigation risks is capped. Thus the value of the TVAF would represent the discount that the financial industry already places on domestic tobacco corporations owing to their litigation risks.

A smooth transition

Changes in ownership of corporations happen all the time. Transfers of corporations, including transfers to or from governmental, generally are carried out in a manner that results in business-as-usual during the transition. In the immediate short term such changes only affect ownership and top-end management. The change is seamless to suppliers, workers, contractors, buyers, end-use consumers and other stakeholders.

Canadians of a certain age will remember that during the purchase by Petro-Canada of BP Canada and Petrofina, the gas continued to flow at the pumps while the Petro-Canada signs were put up. Younger Canadians who buy gas at Petro-Canada might not have even noticed its more recent privatization. Throughout both transitions, Canadian motorists continued to purchase gas for their cars, and the work of the thousands of Petro-Canada employees continued uninterrupted.

The tobacco market can also be transferred to public interest management just as smoothly. As was the case with Petro-Canada, smokers won't notice anything about the pack of cigarettes they buy on the day of the transition. They didn't notice any changes when Imperial Tobacco and Rothman's were sold in 2000. Cigarettes will change, but in the short run they would be sufficiently similar to those currently on the market that smokers would not feel a need or desire to switch to illegal or smuggled cigarettes. As noted earlier, those who work for tobacco corporations would continue to do so at least during the transition period, although some of them (e.g. those involved in marketing and product formulation) would immediately be working towards different goals.

After the transition, a series of changes would occur. Some of these changes would happen immediately. For instance all marketing and promotions would cease, and the people involved would be directed to turn the energies around by 180 degrees. Executives engaged in colluding with smugglers, making product formulation changes that increase consumption, and creating attractive new brand and packaging formats would be re-directed.

Some changes would happen as soon as possible after the transition. For instance packaging would be changed as fast as it could be designed and manufactured. Smokers would still be able to identify their brands in the immediate term, but attractive features would be removed and warnings increased. Counter-marketing and de-branding strategies would be designed, tested and implemented. Industry documents would be released to the public.

And yet some other changes would need to happen literally "yesterday." For instance, any unusual contracts entered into by tobacco corporations in the lead-up period to the transition would be retroactively dissolved by the legislation (without compensation). Assets unusually encumbered or transferred during that period would be re-appropriated without compensation, and any assets the value of which has been reduced or encumbered would be the subject of compensation proceedings against former tobacco corporation directors and domestic and foreign parent corporations. Incentives and compensation could be made available to retailers and others who choose to break their agreements with tobacco corporations before the legislation is proclaimed.

The long-term future for the new system

In the longer term, as tobacco consumption in Canada reaches near-zero levels, vastly lower levels of production would be required. However, it would remain important not to allow foreign tobacco corporations to begin marketing to future generations of Canadians. Thus the public-interest tobacco system would continue to be the sole provider of tobacco products in Canada, and would continue its mandate of reducing tobacco consumption.

It would also assist in the phasing out of tobacco in other countries. There are 191 other member states of the World Health Organization that could all benefit from Canadian success and expertise in phasing out tobacco in their countries. If and when the rest of the world catches up in managing the tobacco epidemic, and the global trade in tobacco is completely eliminated, plans can be made for permanent bans on tobacco production and sales, and the orderly wind-up of the tobacco supply function. Along the way, new opportunities would be created for new lines of work borne of the experience of the planned phase-out of tobacco in Canada, e.g. social marketing of other healthy or socially-worthwhile products and services, such as healthy eating, fitness, environmental protection, social housing, mass transit, etc.

* * *

There are many options for what a health maximizing, consumption reducing tobacco manufacturer could look like. We have attempted to illustrate the range of possibilities by discussing three different options above—the private sector—public interest model, the Crown corporation model, and the government licensing agency model. Again, these models are not policy prescriptions so much as illustrative options.

The broader discussion of this chapter illustrates that it is both possible and desirable to transform the industry. While current tobacco corporations would likely challenge that transformation in court, it is much less likely that they would win. Constitutional legislation can be passed in compliance and furtherance of our international obligations, and financing can be arranged in a number of ways. The transition would be smooth, and the impacts of such a transformation could be positive for the overwhelming majority of stakeholders—smokers and their families, employers, tobacco farmers, taxpayers, and even tobacco corporation shareholders.

And the transformation would allow us—finally—to put in place long-identified measures that would help reduce smoking. These measures have been blocked by tobacco corporations up to now. With this transformation, they would become possible. The following chapter briefly describes some of these measures.

SIX

Taking ownership of the problem

The social problems created by tobacco consumption are complex...innovative legislative solutions are required to address them effectively.
Supreme Court of Canada Justice LaForest [223]

How far do we want to go?

A decade ago, it seemed impossible to imagine a smoke-free Canada. At our current rate of progress, it is almost around the corner — if we can keep tobacco corporations from interfering.

In the mid 1990s, suffering from the setbacks of smuggling, tax rollbacks and unfriendly court judgments, health promoters found it difficult to talk about ambitious goals to reduce smoking. In those years it was hard to track the number of smokers (because the government had suspended surveys for a number of years) or the number of cigarettes smoked (because high rates of smuggling made official sales figures very suspect). The progress that resulted from the 1980s initiatives (including bans on advertising, high taxes and new health warnings) seemed to have stalled.

At the end of the 1990s, federal and provincial health officials and non governmental organizations regrouped to review the framework of the comprehensive plan they had adopted in 1985, the National Strategy to Reduce Tobacco Use. That strategy had set goals to reduce the number of Canadian smokers to 27% of the adult population in 1996 and 24% in 2000,[224] During discussions about renewing the strategy, there was little hope in the air that these targets could be met, let alone that more ambitious targets could be established. The whole notion of setting measurable goals was quietly dropped and the renewed strategy document, *New Directions in Tobacco Control,* published many months later, included no measurable goals.[225]

Health Canada, however, was required by Treasury Board to identify goals when appealed to cabinet for new resources for tobacco programming two years later. Without public consultation, it set a 10 year target for five areas of activity. By 2011, its strategy aimed to:[226]

reduce the number of people who smoke from 25% to 20% of the population;

decrease the number of cigarettes sold by 30%;

increase retailer compliance with laws on tobacco sales to youth from 69% to 80%;

reduce the number of people involuntarily exposed to environmental tobacco smoke in enclosed public spaces;

explore ways to mandate changes to tobacco products to reduce hazards to health.

Most of these goals are being achieved well ahead of schedule. In the five years since the strategy was adopted:

- **Smoking prevalence fell to 20% within four years**
  Statistics Canada surveys report that, in the first half of 2004, the percentage of adults who smoked had fallen to 20% (and 16% in British Columbia).[227] The average rate of decline over the past five years was just under one percentage point per year.

- **Cigarette sales fell by 20% within four years**
  Imperial Tobacco annual reports state that the number of cigarettes sold (which are higher than Statistics Canada's industry reports as

they include estimates of non-reported sales) had decreased by 10 billion cigarettes between 2000 and 2004. The average annual rate of decline over the past five years was 5% per year.[228]

- **Retailer compliance has reached its 80% goal**
Health Canada's survey of retailer compliance with the ban on sales to youth for 2004 reported that the goal of increasing retailer compliance had increased to 80%.[229]

- **The number of Canadians living in smoke-free jurisdictions increased from under 1 million to over 7 million within five years**
Twenty-three percent of Canadians live in jurisdictions where smoking is banned in all indoor public places (without exceptions for bars, casinos or designated smoking rooms) and almost 60% live in places where it is possible to go to restaurants (but possibly not bars or casinos) without being exposed to cigarette smoke.[230] If the legislation now promised by the governments of Ontario, Quebec and Newfoundland is brought into place, the percentage with complete protection will increase to 75%. This will be a 50-fold increase over the protection in place at the beginning of 2000, when British Columbia had the only municipalities with 100% smoke-free laws (the Capital Regional District of Victoria, North Vancouver and White Rock).

Tobacco use in Canada is falling at the fastest rate in history. If the percentage of Canadian smokers and the number of cigarettes sold continue to fall at the same pace as they have over the past five years, then **smoking will disappear in Canada within 15 – 20 years**.

If Health Canada were to renew its goals with new 10 year objectives based on its recent success, it could plan to:

- reduce the number of people who smoke from 20% to 10% of the population by 2015;
- decrease the number of cigarettes sold by 65% by 2015.

Despite these remarkable successes of the past five years, there are few Canadians who are either predicting or planning an end to tobacco. The rosy scenario of these projections is not one that has been put forward by any major health agency or government department.

*There is currently no consensus that tobacco use can be eliminated,
nor even an agreement that ending tobacco use is desirable.*

Progress against tobacco use proceeds by such small increments that many, if not most, tobacco control experts do not accept the elimination of tobacco use as a realistic goal, at least in the foreseeable future. The research and policy communities are more or less silent in projecting schemes to end tobacco use. The journal *Tobacco Control* has published not a single article on the subject in over 10 years.[231]

Even the modern institutional imperative of setting goals and creating mission statements has not encouraged health authorities to identify a timeframe in which the goal of eliminating tobacco use could be entertained. The Canadian government tobacco strategy, for example, sets 10 year goals (aiming to reduce smoking prevalence to 20% and consumption by 30% in 2010), but articulates no longer-term goal to reduce smoking to a lower level.[232]

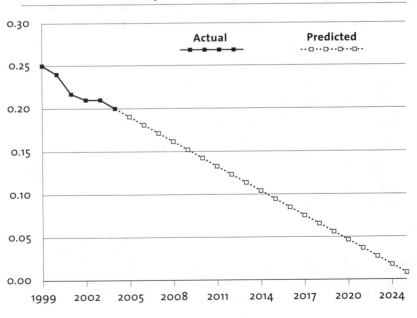

Smoking Rates in Canada
current 5-year trend extrapolated until 2024

In the absence of long-range planning to eliminate tobacco use, long-range public health proposals have emerged which explicitly provide for continued tobacco use. Tobacco corporations aren't the only ones planning for continued high levels of tobacco use (that is to say, greater than 15% prevalence). Some health researchers foresee the need to plan for a long-term nicotine market, where nicotine is provided in safer forms than combustible cigarettes. To do this, some propose that therapeutic drug regulation be liberalized for harm reduction[233] purposes, or that new institutions (such as a special regulatory agency[234] or a tobacco distributor monopoly[235]) be established to manage the supply of cigarettes.

Whatever the goal of their governments or health agencies, Canadian citizens are unequivocal that they want tobacco to go away and that they want governments to do more to make it happen.

In September 2004, the polling firm Environics asked Canadians "Do you strongly agree, somewhat agree, somewhat disagree or strongly disagree that governments should develop new ways to phase out smoking within 25 years?" The answer was clear; 85% of Canadians strongly or somewhat agreed with the statement, and even among smokers, three times as many agreed as disagreed.

"Do you strongly agree, somewhat agree, somewhat disagree or strongly disagree that governments should develop new ways to phase out smoking within 25 years?"[236]

	All	Smokers
Strongly agree	60%	48%
Somewhat agree	25%	28%
Somewhat disagree	6%	10%
Strongly disagree	8%	13%
DK/NA	1%	1%

We do not yet have a way of knowing whether it is possible to eliminate tobacco use, or even how best to reduce it to the lowest levels possible. But we do know that as long as tobacco corporations are working against us, whatever goals we set are harder to reach.

Overcoming the barriers

One reason health authorities and their civil society partners may be reluctant to set ambitious goals is an implicit understanding that, as long as tobacco corporations manage the supply of cigarettes, they may be expected to continue to find ways to overcome the measures that have brought these successes. Our collective memory, as we saw earlier, includes many examples of tobacco corporations being able to stop public measures in their tracks. Those they couldn't stop, they would simply sidestep or adapt and turn to their own advantage (as they did with low-tar cigarettes and measures to prevent young people from smoking).

Another reason for such reluctance may be a concern that the measures we are using may have run their course, and that the smokers who remain are resilient to the effect of high taxes, smoking bans and other encouragements to quit. Those for whom these measures work may have already quit, and those who have not yet quit may need different programs and policies, which we have not yet developed, let alone implemented.

A third reason given against planning to end tobacco use is a belief that it may not be possible for some people to quit. Some special populations (schizophrenics, street people, aboriginal populations) have been identified as less able to overcome nicotine addiction than other Canadians.[237]

None of these reasons suggest that there is a spirit of defeat, a lack of courage or other unwillingness among governments and other health authorities to set ambitious goals for public health. They do suggest an implicit awareness that if we want to keep up our current pace of progress we will need to find a way to stop the companies from thwarting our efforts, to develop new programs and policies and to address the differing needs of smokers.

A non-profit public-interest approach to providing cigarettes can meet these challenges—and do more, besides.

Changing the tobacco market from one where cigarettes are supplied by business corporations programmed to maximize profits to one where cigarettes are supplied by a public interest agency mandated to phase out smoking would be transformative. There would be a profound structural change in the programming and behaviour of those who supplied cigarettes (even if many of the same individuals were involved). The relationships between cigarette makers and governments, communities, and smokers would bear no relationship to our current reality.

With such a profoundly different scenario, it is impossible to detail with any certainty what would happen if the changes we propose were put in place. But the exercise of identifying what would likely happen shows how important (we would argue necessary) this transformation is.

Putting tobacco companies under direct public control could:

- **End the war between big tobacco and public health**
  The struggle between money and health has been fought over cigarettes for so long that it is difficult to imagine that a ceasefire could ever be achieved. Nonetheless, sustainable peace has emerged out of far greater conflicts (the European Union is an example), and governments have, as we have seen, the power and authority to impose a peace on the tobacco conflict.

  The benefits of ending this struggle would be immediately felt. Health Canada and other regulators have been seriously hindered in their ability to implement or even develop new health protection policy because the near-certainty of the tobacco industry launching a court challenge creates a policy chill. As soon as those who make and sell cigarettes share the same goals as health departments, these challenges will end. Measures, like plain packaging or bans on "light" cigarettes, which have been put on indefinite hold could be put into place in quick measures.

- **Tap the secret knowledge of tobacco experts**
  Many of the Canadians with the greatest knowledge about cigarette design and the most advanced marketing research into smoker's behaviour area currently employed by tobacco corporations. By reassigning these individuals to the task of ending smoking, instead of making money, their unique knowledge could be brought into the

effort to save lives. This latent capacity, once released into public service, could help develop new generations of public interventions.

- **Increase innovation**

Many important innovations in tobacco control (like picture-based health warnings) were either initiated or pioneered by Health Canada and other public health agencies. These innovations emerged despite the perceived difficulties of "government innovation." Even higher levels of innovation would be possible if cigarettes were supplied by a public interest tobacco corporation, working in an integrated way with government health agencies and other partners to reduce smoking.

For example, government innovation is currently limited by the barriers on running regulatory experiments. Because federal law applies equally across Canada the measures that are put in place for one region have to be put in place for all regions. This makes it difficult to test-market innovations, to compare approaches or to experiment with approaches. A tobacco company that shared the same goals as government would be free to use its administrative authority to research, experiment and develop new approaches.

- **Meet the needs of special populations**

Not all smokers are the same. Tobacco companies know this, which is why they package essentially the same cigarette to appeal to different segments of the market. A tobacco company that was trying to get smokers to quit could use this ability to tailor its de-marketing of cigarettes to different populations.

For example, many health programs currently use the "stages of change" approach[238] to address the different needs or different willingness of smokers to move towards quitting. This approach separates smokers into five categories: those who are not thinking seriously about quitting and are not interested in any kind of help (pre-contemplation), those who are thinking about quitting sometime within the next six months (contemplation), those who are getting ready to quit (preparation), those who have recently quit (action) and those who have quit and are staying quit (maintenance). A tobacco manufacturer trying to move smokers into quitting and trying to improve the ability of ex-smokers to stay quit may find ways of using these distinctions to support the work of those running programs to assist quitting.

There are other ways in which the special needs of some populations could be reached. Smoking rates are often very heavy among disadvantaged groups (like the homeless or mentally ill). A tobacco company that has the responsibility to helping such smokers quit (and not the responsibility to exploit their disadvantage to increase the profits of shareholders) would have the authority, responsibility and economic ability to provide free or heavily-subsidized nicotine substitutes to these communities with special needs.

- **Meet the needs of smokers**
Public measures to reduce smoking are, generally speaking, population health interventions. That is to say, they are focused on community-wide changes, rather than focusing on individual behaviour change (although the community change includes the aggregate of many individual changes). Because of this, governments are often seen to be doing things *to* smokers (like increasing taxes or reducing the places where people can smoke) instead of doing things *for* smokers (like providing help in quitting). The reasons governments take this approach is because it is both more effective and more economic than, for example, setting up smoking cessation clinics (although some governments, like the United Kingdom Department of Health, have invested heavily in a stop smoking service[239]).

Once the market is transformed into one where those supplying cigarettes are integrated members of a public health community, there would be a vastly greater shared ability to meet the varying needs of smokers. Those who did not want to quit could be provided with constant and supportive information about reducing the harm to their health through the use of less harmful products, as well as incentives to use those products. Those who wanted to quit could be provided with constant and supportive information about quitting, as well as direct assistance tailored to their own preferences.

Smokers would no longer receive conflicting information from cigarette suppliers and their physician or local health unit.

Comparison of proposed model with current situation

Canada's current comprehensive strategy	Public interest tobacco industry
RELATIONSHIP BETWEEN SUPPLIER AND HEALTH AUTHORITIES	
Antagonistic	Integrated and collaborative
PRODUCTS SOLD	
Branded tobacco products (other products that deliver nicotine are regulated under different authorities)	Tobacco products progressively designed, manufactured, packaged and delivered in ways that facilitate quitting and discourage uptake
ASSUMPTIONS (STATED AND UNSTATED)	
It is not feasible or practicable to end tobacco use	It is possible to end tobacco use once there is no financial interest in maintaining it
Supply-side approaches should not be used	Tobacco companies will continue to undermine tobacco control measures and will sustain smoking
Tobacco corporations do not have a legitimate role in the development of public health strategies to reduce smoking	Trade agreements do not prohibit establishment of monopolies if doing so achieves justifiable health objectives and if compensation is provided
	Acquiring tobacco supply increases capacity to innovate to achieve public health goals
COMPLETE PUBLIC INTEREST CONTROL OVER	
	Distribution, promotion, packaging, pricing, product design, manufacture, retailing
SOME PUBLIC INTEREST CONTROL OVER	
Promotion, packaging, pricing, product design	

Comparison of proposed model with current situation

Canada's current comprehensive strategy	Public interest tobacco industry
MARKET INSTRUMENT	
Multinational corporations	Non-profit tobacco monopoly
Domestic tobacco companies	
HEALTH GOAL	
Reduce mortality and morbidity associated with tobacco	End mortality and morbidity associated with tobacco
POLICY GOAL	
Reduce the demand for cigarettes	Phase-out tobacco use
Protect public from second-hand smoke	
STRATEGIES EMPLOYED	
Regulated sale of tobacco product (restrictions on advertising, mandatory health warnings)	Continued measures from comprehensive strategy as appropriate
Higher prices through taxes	Public interest control over complete tobacco supply chain
Health promotion	Integration of cigarette design, manufacture and supply with programs and policies to reduce smoking
Smoke-free indoor work and public places	
Curbs on smuggling	
ANALAGOUS TO	
Consumer protection law	Public water, sanitation and health systems
TOBACCO INDUSTRY TRIES TO:	
Maximize profits within a regulated market.	Help smokers quit as quickly as possible and prevent tobacco uptake
TOBACCO WORKERS DIRECTED TO:	
Increase profits for tobacco corporations	Help smokers quit as quickly as possible and prevent tobacco uptake

- **Resolve the ambiguity of government's intentions**

  A system as vast and as complex as government will almost inevitably include a number of inconsistent policies and incoherent practices.

  This is certainly true for tobacco. For example, the federal government which, with one agency (Health Canada) tries to reduce the number of people who smoke, invests in tobacco companies with another (the Canada Pension Plan). Concern about government's apparent ambivalence to tobacco may weigh down public willingness to adopt new measures. Not infrequently, Canadians complain "if the government really wanted to get rid of tobacco, they would ban it," or "the government doesn't really want to get rid of tobacco because they are so dependent on cigarette taxes."

  The proposal for the purchase of tobacco companies and the re-direction of their operations to meet health goals would create a far higher degree of policy coherence. The role of high cigarette prices/taxes would be clearly articulated in legislation as a way of financing the removal of tobacco companies and of discouraging use. Legislated goals on reducing smoking, with the goal of phasing out both smoking and cigarette taxes, would clarify that there is no ambivalence about maintaining cigarette tax income or about ending tobacco use.

Create a more cohesive society

One of the difficulties of governments is that they must represent the needs of all citizens, even when those needs are clearly at cross-purposes.

It's not only politicians who feel the tension between conflicting social groups. Today's cigarette market pits the specific economic interests of tobacco farmers and employees of cigarette companies against those of the general economic, social and health interest of the community. This conflict can be resolved by bringing these citizens together in collective purpose. Tobacco farmers and tobacco workers know that their long-term employment prospects are not good. They also know that their economic well-being is tied to a product which is, gently put, controversial. A planned tobacco phase-out program would be able to include measures for an orderly and dignified transition of these workers into other sectors. No longer would the economic needs of these Canadians be pitted against the health needs of others.

Tobacco policy measures — what is good enough?

Some may ask "Do we really need to transform the industry? Can't we just continue with existing policy instruments?" As we saw, we have had some successes. However, a decline in the number of Canadians smoking from 6 million to 5 million after 40 years of effort does not exactly justify resting on our laurels.

It is clear that tobacco consumption isn't going down by itself. It is going down because it responds to the application of policy instruments. If policy instruments are made more comprehensive or applied more rigorously, then consumption will go down further. When policy instruments are removed or even just relaxed, consumption will level out or increase.[240] There is a direct relationship between the application of policy instruments, and the consumption levels of tobacco. If we want to continue the current declines in consumption rates, we need to continue to apply policy instruments more comprehensively and more rigorously.

Yet some policy instruments can only be used to a certain point. They tend to have a declining rate of return. For instance, when in-store promotion is curtailed as much as possible, then no further gains will be made from that instrument. When packaging contains as large warning labels and as little brand content as possible, then no further gains will be made from that instrument. When prices are so high that reductions in licit sales are matched by increases in illicit sales — even with enhanced funding for enforcement — then further increases will not reduce consumption. So we need to be able to use additional policy instruments. Industry transformation is one such instrument.

If the industry is transformed by being placed in public interest hands, a much fuller spectrum of policy measures can be used, as we saw above.

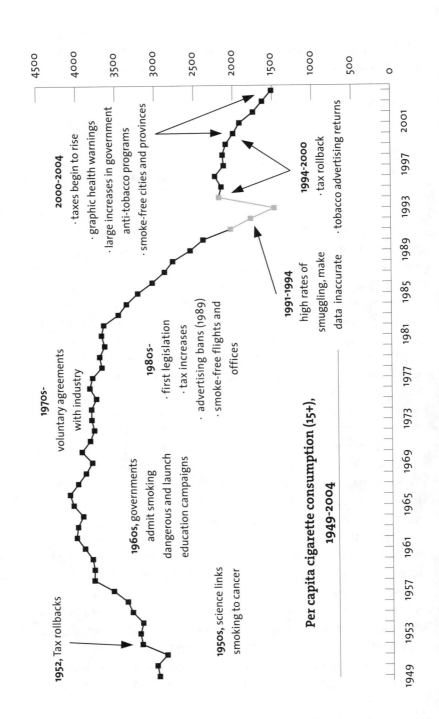

Per capita cigarette consumption (15+), 1949-2004

1952, Tax rollbacks

1950s, science links smoking to cancer

1960s, governments admit smoking dangerous and launch education campaigns

1970s- voluntary agreements with industry

1980s-
· first legislation
· tax increases
· advertising bans (1989)
· smoke-free flights and offices

1991-1994
high rates of smuggling, make data inaccurate

1994-2000
· tax rollback
· tobacco advertising returns

2000-2004
· taxes begin to rise
· graphic health warnings
· large increases in government anti-tobacco programs
· smoke-free cities and provinces

This helps overcome the limits on policy measures that is imposed by the policy chill or court decisions that result from private-sector challenges to public health law. In 1995 the tobacco industry's challenge of the *Tobacco Products Control Act* resulted in the striking down of several of the Act's key advertising provisions.[241] A new *Tobacco Act* was subsequently adopted in 1997, and the industry has now also taken this one to court.[242] Clearly the tobacco industry, through litigation (not to mention lobbying) imposes limits on what policy instruments can be used, and to what extent they can be used. And the category of "what can be used" is limited.

Is "what can be used" good enough? Is what the industry will allow us to use good enough? No.

We need to have the *best possible* policy measures for reducing tobacco consumption. We need to have the *best possible* measures for preventing uptake. We need to have the *best possible* measures for supporting smokers in their efforts to quit. And we need to have no interference, no counter-messages, of any sort, direct or indirect. Anything less than the best is not good enough for tobacco victims, present and future. Anything less than the best is not good enough for their families. We owe it to them to obtain and use the best possible measures.

And it should be clear by now that with our current for-profit, consumption-expanding industry, we don't have the best possible measures. Indeed, we *can't* have the best possible measures. And what we do have, in plentiful supply, is interference and counter-messages.

Plan for the unexpected

Some would say removing the for-profit corporations from the manufacture of tobacco is a good idea, but impossible. Lots of things are impossible until they happen: the four-minute mile; the fall of the Berlin wall; the end of Apartheid, putting a man on the moon; and a baby's first steps. The fact is that corporations have been broken up, bought out, and entirely removed from many sectors in the past, many times, for hundreds of years. The fact is that many positive achievements look impossible until they are done.

Many of the achievements we have already made with tobacco looked impossible at one time.

In today's policy climate, with the adoption of the Framework Convention on Tobacco Control, it is difficult to imagine societies being willing to allow tobacco to be sold with virtually no controls, to imagine people smoking in buses, airplanes, university classrooms and doctor's offices. Yet these were the circumstances in Canada only 20 years ago.

It is equally—or more—difficult to imagine a House of Commons poised to ban cigarettes. Yet this was the circumstance a century ago.

Proposals considered "politically unfeasible" thirty years ago (like banning advertising) are now codified in international treaties. Ideas once dismissed as "unacceptable" to Canadian communities (like smoke-free bars) are now well on their way to becoming the norm across Canada.

Policy in areas other than public health has experienced similarly tumultuous change (only 20 years ago, Petro Canada and Air Canada were owned by government, and foreign investments were subject to more stringent government review). In light of our own political life experience, dismissing any proposal as being too unrealistic to warrant consideration is arguably short-sighted.

Circumstances may demand that governments have a new way of managing tobacco supply

Although the push for change to how tobacco is managed may come from public health agents, the impetus that moves governments to implement these changes may come from very different sources. It may be the collapse (perhaps due to lawsuits) of tobacco corporations or the decision of tobacco corporations to withdraw from a market that requires governments to develop mechanisms to manage the supply of cigarettes.

A crisis in the tobacco market is an opportunity for new ways of managing tobacco. Recent experiences suggest that such crises do occur:

- In 1990, the collapse and reformation of the soviet economy resulted in a shortage of cigarettes in Russia, and anxious smokers expressed their concern through riots and blockades. President Mikhail Gorbachev, in need of a solution, asked for foreign help, and the American tobacco companies airlifted 34 billion cigarettes.[243] This market crisis was the transition point where control of Russia's tobacco market was transferred from government control to that of tobacco transnationals.

- In the late 1990s, a Canadian provincial government was told by tobacco corporations that they would "pull out" of the province if a certain policy initiative was implemented.[244] In the absence of a backup plan, that government chose not to implement the measure rather than find an alternative way to manage the cigarette market.

- During the early 1990s, the Canadian government intent to increase the price of tobacco through taxation was undermined by high volumes of smuggling. The perception that up to 30% of cigarettes smoked in Canada were illegally-sold and purchased, and that the increase in smuggling would have knock-on effects on crime rates and violence prompted the Canadian government to regain control by reducing taxes in most regions of the country. Unlike other smuggling scenarios, where the cigarettes are imported from other countries, the cigarettes smuggled into Canada at this time originated in Canada. Had the government had alternatives to control the complete supply of tobacco products, more options would have been available.

- In September 1995, the Supreme Court of Canada struck down the **Tobacco Products Control Act** and the government was caught (or at least appeared to be caught) flat-footed, without options to respond to the court decision other than by amending the laws on tobacco advertising. The Court ruled that the government had not demonstrated that it was necessary to infringe on the charter-protected expression rights of the tobacco companies in order to protect youth from inducements to smoke. Had the government developed ways of **managing** the tobacco market (as opposed to **regulating** the tobacco market) to meet this objective, they may have been able to reply to the court decision with stronger measures, not, as it turned out, a weaker law. Of course, if a public-interest tobacco manufacturer had already been in place, the law would never have been challenged in the first place.

- On March 21, 2003, Illinois judge Nicholas Byron ruled that Philip Morris/Altria deceived Illinois smokers of Marlboro Lights by marketing that brand as being safer than full-flavor cigarettes, and levied a US$10 billion fine against the company. When the appeal bond was set at $12 billion, Philip Morris/Altria threatened bankruptcy.[245] Unprepared for this outcome, several states began to pass legislation which capped bonds to ensure that tobacco companies could keep operating.[246]

- In the summer of 2004, JTI-Macdonald asked to be placed under bankruptcy protection, saying it could not afford to make the payment demanded by the Quebec Ministry of Revenue as compensation for taxes that were unpaid as a result of the company's involvement with smuggling in the early 1990s.[247]

Some of these events suggest there are scenarios under which governments can acquire tobacco operations at little or no cost. All of them suggest that governments should be actively planning ways of putting tobacco supply under public management.

We may be forced to act. Tobacco corporations could well go out of business because of their heavy litigation liabilities. On the other hand, we may not be forced to act. The existing industry may just go on as it is doing today for decades.

It's our choice — and our responsibility

We're at a crossroads. The path we are on we share with a for-profit industry that limits policies, creates extra costs and causes more deaths. We can change course, increase cooperation and reduce costs, disease and death. We can take either road. Every day we don't chose the healthy road, more people die.

So, while a positive, pro-health industry is ours if we choose it, we also have the choice of keeping the same old industry that we have to-day—the same old industry that lies to the public and to their elected representatives, works to create new addicts and retain old ones, lobbies and litigates to undermine public health measures, breaks the law, and seeks to expand sales of a deadly product.

More tobacco or less tobacco—a choice we face every day

We know that tobacco will be with us in the short term, and likely the medium term. There is no doubt that tobacco will be sold in Canada in coming years. The question we face is who should be selling that tobac-co. The answer to the question of *who sells* will also determine *how much* gets sold. It is true that even a small amount of tobacco being sold will kill people. But a for-profit industry will sell more of it, and a for-health industry will sell less. The more tobacco is sold, the more Canadians will get sick and die. When less tobacco is sold, fewer Canadians will get sick and die. We could term the difference in deaths between these two sce-narios the "for-profit death increment."

The question of who should sell tobacco is one we face every day. It is not a question we can escape by pretending it is not there. The question is there, right in front of us—today and every day. Every day we pretend that question is not there, or that we don't have to answer it, is another day we allow for-profit tobacco corporations to continue to expand their markets and recruit new smokers. They are successful in this; they recruit another 200 Canadian youth every day.[248]

Every day we allow that to happen, we guarantee that more tobacco will be sold to future generations. Every day we allow that to happen, we condemn more of our children and our grandchildren, and their loved ones, to cancer, emphysema, heart disease, and finally a premature, trag-ic death.

We deliberately say "every day" because the fact is that even one day makes an enormous difference. Every day, over 125 Canadians die from tobacco. What if we had transformed the tobacco industry 40 years ago, when the evidence of tobacco's health impacts was mounting? How many people who have died from tobacco-related illness since then would be alive today? How many families would still be complete?

It's up to us — not Big Tobacco — to do things differently

As discussed earlier in this book, in trying to sell a larger number of cigarettes (which will kill a larger number of people) tobacco corporations are not being evil. They are no more guilty of wrongdoing than a ball is guilty of rolling down a slope. Corporations are not capable of being evil, and they are not capable of being good; they are inanimate instruments incapable of any moral judgment or culpability. They have no choice in the matter.

Ultimately, corporations are simple, rule-driven instruments. We can thus predict what a corporation will do in a given situation. Tobacco corporations won't change their behaviour in ways that reduce tobacco use, because they can't change their behaviour in this way. They will go on to maximize share values, profit and tobacco sales in the future. We know this.

We are the only ones who can change tobacco industry behaviour. Corporations can't and won't change it. Their directors and managers can't and won't change it. Only we can. We make a decision on this subject every day, whether we choose to acknowledge it or not, whether it is an explicit decision or a tacit decision.

Because we are the only ones who can make the decision, and because we do in fact make the decision every day, it is not just our *choice* what the future tobacco industry and the future tobacco death rate will look like. It is our *responsibility*.

Key indicators of progress against tobacco

	1965	1970	1975	1981
Percentage of Canadians over 15 years of age who smoke				
	49.5	46.5	44.5	39.5
Percentage of Canadians aged 15-19 who smoke				
	46	49.5	49.5	43.5
Number of Canadians over 15 who smoke				
	6.5 mln	6.9 mln	7.6 mln	7.6 mln
Number of cigarettes sold				
	52.9 bln	58.4 bln	64.3 bln	71.3 bln
Number of cigarettes per capita (over 15) sold				
	4,049	3,940	3,754	3,685

	1985	1990	1995	2000	2004
Percentage of Canadians over 15 years of age who smoke					
	34	31	26	24	20
Percentage of Canadians aged 15-19 who smoke					
	27.5	21	24	25	20
Number of Canadians over 15 who smoke					
	6.9 mln	6.8 mln	6.1 mln	6 mln	5.1 mln
Number of cigarettes sold					
	65.8 bln	53.8 bln	50.8 bln	49.5 bln	39.6 bln
Number of cigarettes per capita (over 15) sold					
	3,222	2,444	2,159	1,996	1,510

Sources:
1965-1986: A Critical Review of Canadian Survey Data on Tobacco Use, Atti-tudes and Knowledge, Health and Welfare Canada, 1988; 1990: Canada's Health Promotion Survey 1990: Technical Report, Health and Welfare Canada, 1993; 1995 General Social Survey, Statistics Canada; 2000, 2005 Canadian Tobacco Use Monitoring Survey, 2000

Chapter 1

1   D. Kessler. *A Question of Intent: A Great American Battle with a Deadly Industry.* New York: Public Affairs, 2001, p. 392.

2   *House of Commons Debates.* June 17, 1963, p. 1213–1214.

3   Associated Press. "Giving up Smoking Good, Bad and Awful." *St. Paul Dispatch.* June 19, 1963. Found at Philip Morris document 2025028937B.

4   *House of Commons Debates.* November 26, 1963, p. 5108. Found at Philip Morris document 2024991699.

5   Health and Welfare Canada. *A Critical Review of Canadian Survey Data on Tobacco Use, Attitudes and Knowledge.* Ottawa, 1988.

6   Health Canada. *Canadian Tobacco Use Monitoring Survey.* Ottawa, 2004.

7   Ibid.

8   Health and Welfare Canada. *A Critical Review of Canadian Survey Data on Tobacco Use, Attitudes and Knowledge.* Ottawa, 1988

9   Imperial Tobacco. *Annual Reports.* Montreal, 1965 to 2004.

10   E.M. Makomaski Illing and M.J. Kaiserman. "Mortality Attributable to Tobacco Use in Canada and its Regions, 1994 and 1996." *Chronic Diseases in Canada.* Volume 20, No. 3, 1999.

11   M.E. Palko. *The Canadian Smoking and Health Programme.* Found at Philip Morris document 1005154086.

12   A.D. McCormick. *Confidential Memo, Smoking and Health.* 28th November 1963, found at Philip Morris document 100427884.

13   Imperial Tobacco. *Brief to the Standing Committee on Health.* (Isabelle Committee), 1969.

14   J.L. Mercier. *Testimony to the Standing Committee on Health.* November 1987.

15 Imperial Tobacco Canada. *Problem*. Document taken from Guildford depository, beginning page 102694872.

16 M.H. Bilimoria. *Ames Mutagenicity of Mainstream and Sidestream Smoke Condensates*. Imperial Tobacco Canada Research Report T-7708. 1981.

17 U.S. Department of Health and Human Services. *The Health Consequences of Involuntary Smoking: A Report of the surgeon General*. Atlanta, Georgia, 1986.

18 See an example of this strategy in Canada at S. Glantz. *Ventilation Hoax: Hired Guns. Profile of Theodore Sterling and Associates*, Tobacco Scam. http://www.tobaccoscam.ucsf.edu/vent/vent_hg_internal.cfm. Accessed March 21, 2005.

19 A chronology of the campaign the industry ran against smoking bans can be found in Physicians for a Smoke-Free Canada. *Behind the Scenes. How the Companies Tried to Use 'Ventilation' Solutions to Block Restrictions on Smoking*. http://www.smoke-free.ca/documents/ventilation.htm. Accessed March 21, 2005.

20 Imasco. *History of Activities in Canada*. October 17, 1978. Found at Philip Morris document 1005144957.

21 Philip Morris. *Plain Packaging Would Violate Canada's International Trade Obligations*. May 19, 1994.

22 N. Francey and S. Chapman. "Operation Berkshire: the International Tobacco Companies' Conspiracy." *British Medical Journal*, 2000;321:371-374.

23 Ibid.

24 D. Durden. *Discussion Paper on Background Issues, Conclusions and a Possible Plan for Countermeasure Development Efforts by SAWP*. RJReynolds Document 506206748-57, cited at page 506206751.

25 J. Paraskevas. "Saskatchewan scores resounding victory over tobacco giant." *Edmonton Journal*, January 20, 2005.

26 M.E. Goldberg et al. "When Packages Can't Speak: Possible Impacts of Plain and Generic Packaging of Tobacco Products". Expert Panel Report prepared at the request of Health Canada. Ottawa, 1995.

27 M. Kennedy. "Tobacco companies fight federal rules: Retailers asked to join campaign against plan to curb youth smoking." *The Calgary Herald*. May 1, 1999.

28 Anonymous. "How Big Tobacco Rules Canada." *Eye Magazine*. December 16, 1999.

29 www.mychoice.ca. Accessed March 25, 2005.

30 Philip Morris USA. Health Issues. http://www.philipmorrisusa.com/en/health_issues/default.asp. Accessed March 15, 2005.

31 K. Clegg-Smith and M. Wakefield. "The name of Philip Morris to sit on 28 million school desks." *Tobacco Control*. 2001.

32 M.C. Farrelly. "Getting to the truth: evaluating national tobacco countermarketing campaigns." *American Journal of Public Health*. 2002 June 92 (6): 901-7.

33 A list of agencies supported by Imperial Tobacco Canada Ltd., including these three agencies, is provided on www.imperialtobacco.ca. Accessed March 15, 2005.

34 Imasco. *History of activities in Canada*. October 17, 1978. Found at Philip Morris document 1005144957.

35 J.B. Claxton. *Smoking and Health in Canada*. 1976. Philip Morris documents 1005145136.

36 Anonymous. *Minutes of BAT Research Conference Held at Hilton Head Island*. 1986. Brown & Williamson documents 500013480.

37 R.E. Griffith. *Report to Executive Committee*. July 1965. Brown & Williamson document 680204131.

38 Ames test described in *Minutes of the BAT Biological Conference*.1984. Massachusetts document 401035491.

39 Anonymous. *Minutes of the BAT Biological Conference*.1984. Massachusetts document 401035491.

40 R. Bexon. *Paper 6: New Brand Development, Post-Light*. 1984. Imperial Tobacco via British American Tobacco documents 400993243.

41 Physicians for a Smoke-Free Canada. *Smokers of "light" cigarettes Findings from the Canadian Tobacco Use Monitoring Survey*, 2004.

42 A. Landman et al. "Tobacco industry youth smoking prevention programs: protecting the industry and hurting tobacco control," *American Journal of Public Health*. June 2002, Vol. 92, No. 6, p. 917-930.

43 R. Pollay. *Export A Ads are Extremely Expert, Eh?* Filter tips, available at www.smoke-free.ca.

44 R. Cunningham. *Smoke and Mirrors, the Canadian Tobacco War*. International Development Research Council, Ottawa, 1996.

45 *Ibid*.

46 *Ibid*.

47 G. Atidion. *The Structure of Drug Prohibition in International Law and in Canadian Law*. Doctoral Thesis, University of Montreal, School of Criminology, 1999.

48 R. Cunningham. *Smoke and Mirrors, the Canadian Tobacco War*. International Development Research Council, Ottawa, 1996.

49 Imperial Tobacco Canada Ltd. *Annual Report*.1966.

50 Imperial Tobacco Canada Ltd. and Imasco Ltd. *Annual Reports*. 1977-2004.

51 R. Borland. "A Strategy for Controlling the Marketing of Tobacco Products: a Regulated Market Model." *Tobacco Control*. 2003; 12: 374-82.

52   Strategic Counsel. *A presentation to IMASCO – May 1998*. ITL Exhibit 607 from JTI Macdonald versus the Attorney General of Canada.

Chapter 2

53   Non-Smoker's Rights Association. *Campaign for Tobacco Industry Denormalization*. November 1, 2004.

54   J. MacKay. *The Tobacco Epidemic Amongst Young People*. World Congress on Medicine and Health. August 2000.

55   J. Micklethwait and A. Wooldridge. *The Company: a Short History of a Revolutionary Idea*. Modern Library, New York, , 2003, p. 20.

56   For further discussions of the evolution of the business corporation, see:

J. Bakan. *The Corporation. The pathological pursuit of profit and power*. Viking Canada, 2004, chapter 1 and sources cited therein;

J. Micklethwait and A. Wooldridge, *The Company: a Short History of a Revolutionary Idea*. Modern Library, New York, , 2003, chapters 1 – 5;

The Aurora Institute. *The Corporation Inside and Out*. available at www.aurora.ca.

57   J. Micklethwait and A. Wooldridge. *The Company: a Short History of a Revolutionary Idea*. Modern Library, New York, , 2003, p. 49.

58   Corporations Canada. *Frequently Asked Questions*. http://strategis.ic.gc.ca.

59   J. Bakan. *The Corporation. The Pathological Pursuit of Profit and Power*. Viking Canada, 2004, p. 13. and J. Micklethwait and A. Wooldridge, *The Company: a Short History of a Revolutionary Idea*, Modern Library, New York, 2003, p. 51.

60   J. Micklethwait and A. Wooldridge, *The Company: a Short History of a Revolutionary Idea*. Modern Library, New York, 2003, p.46.

61   Ibid. and J. Bakan. *The Corporation. The Pathological Pursuit of Profit and Power*. Viking Canada, 2004, p. 13-14.

62   J. Bakan. *The Corporation. The Pathological Pursuit of Profit and Power*. Viking Canada, 2004, p. 14.

63   The Aurora Institute discusses nine such characteristics in *The Corporation Inside and Out*. http://www.aurora.ca/guide.php.

64   *Canada Business Corporations Act* (R.S.C. 1985, c. C-44), s.122.(1)(a). A provincial example is *Ontario's Business Corporations Act* R.S.O. 1990, Chapter B.16, s. 134(1)(a).

65   J.A. VanDuzer. *The Law of Partnerships and Corporations*. Irwin Law, Toronto, 2003, pp. 271-2.

66   C. Crook. "The Good Company. A Survey of Corporate Social Responsibility." *The Economist*, 2005;374:8410.

67 Notably, corporations in Germany also involve employees in their accountability structures. Large German corporations are required to have a two-tier board of directors, involving a management board overseeing day-to-day manage-rial issues, and a supervisory board performing strategic oversight. This supervi-sory board, in firms of over 2000 employees, must be comprised half of share-holder representatives and half of employee representatives.

68 *Articles of Incorporation Licensed to Kill Inc.* www. Licensedtokill.biz, Accessed March 3, 2004.

69 The case of small corporations, in which managers are the owners, is not considered in this book, as it is not generally relevant to the tobacco industry.

70 See for example, the shareholder motions of the Interfaith Center on Corporate Responsibility. www.iccr.org/shareholder/proxy_book04/04statuschart.php Ac-cessed March 15, 2005.

71 Canadian Pension Plan Investment Board. *Proxy Voting Principles and Guidelines*. February 2004, p. 22. www.cppib.ca. Accessed March 8, 2004.

72 Canada Pension Plan Investment Board. *How We Invest*. http://www.cppib.ca/how/index.html Accessed February 27, 2004.

73 Industry Canada. *Lobbyists Registration Act - Annual Report 2003-2004*. Ottawa, 2004.

74 G. Hein. "Interest Group Litigation and Canadian Democracy." *Choices*. Institute for Research on Public Policy, March, 2000, pp.8-9.

75 Canada Revenue Agency. IT-104R3 - Deductibility of Fines or Penalties. Ottawa, 2004.

76 Cited in J. Bakan. *The Corporation. The pathological pursuit of profit and power*. Viking Canada, 2004, p. 14.

77 *Ibid.*, p. 34.

78 J. Collin and A. Gilmore. "Corporate (Anti) Social (Ir)Responsibility: Transnational Tobacco Companies and the Attempted Subversion of Global Health Policy." *Global Social Policy* 2(3), p. 354-360.

79 D. Spurgeon. "University is criticized for accepting tobacco money." *British Medical Journal*, 8 March 2003, vol 326, p. 519.

80 J. Collin and A. Gilmore. "Corporate (Anti) Social (Ir)Responsibility: Transnational Tobacco Companies and the Attempted Subversion of Global Health Policy." *Global Social Policy* 2(3), p. 359.

81 N. Hirschhorn. "Corporate social responsibility and the tobacco industry: hope or hype?" *Tobacco Control*. 2004;13:447-453.

82 Environics. *Focus Canada 2004-3*. Toronto, 2004.

Chapter 3

83   U.S. Department of Health and Human Services. *Reducing Tobacco Use. A report of the Surgeon General.* Atlanta, Georgia, 2000.

84   World Health Organization, Resolutions 33.31 (1980), 39.14 (1986), 43.16 (1990), 45.20 (1992), 48.11 (1995). Geneva, 1980-1995.

85   World Health Organization. *Draft Framework Convention on Tobacco Control.* Resolution 56.1. Geneva, 2003.

86   The World Bank. *Curbing the epidemic: governments and the economics of tobacco control.* Tobacco Control, 1999: 8: 196-201.

87   H. Saffer. "Tobacco Advertising and Promotion," in *Tobacco Control in Developing Countries.* Oxford University Press, 2000.

88   Centers for Disease Control and Prevention. "Strategies for reducing exposure to environmental tobacco smoke, increasing tobacco-use cessation, and reducing initiation in communities and health care systems." *MMWR Morbidity and Mortality Weekly Report.* 2000: 49: 1-11.

89   M.J. Kaiserman et al. *The Evaluation of Canada's Health Warning Messages: 18 Month Follow-Up.* Health Canada, Ottawa, 2004.

90   D. Hammond et al. "The Impact of Cigarette Warning Labels and Smoke-Free Bylaws on Smoking Cessation: Evidence from Former Smokers." *Canadian Journal of Public Health*, 2004 May-Jun; 95(3):201-4.

91   World Health Organization. Resolution A56/8/ Rev.1, May 2003.

92   M. Aquilino et al. "Approaches to tobacco Control: the Evidence Base." *European Journal of Dental Education.* 8 (Suppl. 4): 11-17.

93   Health Canada. *New Directions for Tobacco Control in Canada. A National Strategy.* Prepared by: Steering Committee of the National Strategy to Reduce Tobacco Use in Canada in Partnership with Advisory Committee on Population Health. Ottawa, 1997.

94   P. Jha and F.J. Chaloupka, *Curbing the Epidemic, Governments and the Economics of Tobacco Control.* World Bank, 1999.

95   M. Tilson. *A Critical Analysis of Youth Access Laws.* Canadian Cancer Society, September 2002.

96   P. Jha and F.J. Chaloupka. "The Economics of Global Tobacco Control." *British Medical Journal.* 2000;321:358-361.

97   Agriculture Canada. *Evaluation of the Tobacco Diversification Plan (Tobacco Transition Adjustment Initiative and Alternative Enterprise Initiative) Executive Report.* Ottawa, 1990.

98   Competition Bureau of Canada. *Annual Report on Competition Developments in Canada, April 1, 1999 to March 31, 2000.* Presented to the Organization for Economic Cooperation and Development.

99   Alberta Statutes and Regulations. *Prevention of Youth Tobacco Use Act*, Chapter P-22.

100 Agriculture Canada. *Plan Aimed at Helping Tobacco Producers and Communities Move Toward Reduced Production*. Ottawa, May 4, 2004.

101 Canadian Cancer Society. *Retail Sale of Tobacco Products on Prince Edward Island, a Brief Submitted to the Legislative Standing Committee on Social Development*. Charlottetown, 2004.

102 E. Gulbrandsen and S. Skeath. *Would Big Tobacco Have Been Better?: the Social Welfare Implications of Antitrust Action in the Presence of Negative Externalities*. Wellesley, Massachusetts: Wellesley College, 1999, p. 4.

103 J. McKay and M. Eriksen. *The Tobacco Atlas*. World Health Organization, Geneva, 2003.

104 Competition Bureau of Canada. *Annual Report on Competition Developments in Canada, April 1, 1999 to March 31, 2000*. Presented to the Organization for Economic Cooperation and Development.

105 Judith McKay and Michael Eriksen. *The Tobacco Atlas*. World Health Organization, Geneva, 2003.

106 P.L. Barnes. *Expanding PM's presence in China's Tobacco Sector*. Philip Morris Document 2077415839-2077415849.

107 A.A. Yurekli. *Tobacco and China. A Complex Challenge*. World Bank Ministerial Level Economics of Tobacco Control Seminar. Beijing, 2000.

108 B. Fisher. "The Power of Regionalism. Capitalizing on its Strength in Local Markets. British American Tobacco has Crafted a Formidable Global Entity." *Tobacco Reporter*, June 2001.

109 Japan Tobacco. *Annual Report*. 2003.

110 Agriculture Canada. *Plan Aimed at Helping Tobacco Producers and Communities Move Toward Reduced Production*. Press release. Ottawa, May 4, 2004.

111 World Trade Organization. *Thailand – Restrictions on Importation of and Internal Taxes on Cigarettes, Report of the Panel adopted on 7 November 1990* (DS10/R – 37S/200).

112 Competition Bureau of Canada. *Annual Report on Competition Developments in Canada, April 1, 1999 to March 31, 2000*. Presented to the Organization for Economic Cooperation and Development.

113 Centre de Documentation et d'Information sur le Tabac. *Le Marché du Tabac en 2002*. http://www.cdit.fr/pdf/tn24.pdf Accessed February 25, 2004.

114 *Ibid*.

115 Imperial Tobacco. *Declaration*. Imperial Tobacco Ltd. vs. Attorney General of Canada, document no. 500-05-031332-974.

116 S. Ugen. "Bhutan: the World's Most Advanced Tobacco Control Nation?" *Tobacco Control*. 2003 Dec;12(4):431-3.

117 R. Cunningham. *Smoke and Mirrors, the Canadian Tobacco War*. International Development Research Council, Ottawa, 1996, p. 289.

118 Senate of Canada. *Report of the Senate Special Committee on Illegal Drugs.* Ottawa, 2003.

119 P. Jha and F.J. Chaloupka, *Curbing the Epidemic*, Governments and the Economics of Tobacco Control. World Bank, 1999. p. 57.

120 Subcommittee on Commerce, Trade and Consumer Protection. *Can Tobacco Cure Smoking. A Review of Tobacco Harm Reduction*, Hearing before the Commerce subcommittee. June 3, 2003, p. 57.

121 M. Kaufman. "Surgeon General Favors Tobacco Ban." *Washington Post*, June 4, 2003; Page A01.

122 Lancet. "How Do You Sleep at Night, Mr. Blair." *Lancet*, Vol. 362, December 6, 2003. p. 1865.

123 BBC. "UK Ministers Urged to Ban Tobacco." *BBC News*. Friday, 5 December, 2003, 08:24 GMT. Accessed 22 February 2004.

124 The China Daily. "Bhutan becomes first nation to ban tobacco sales," *China Daily*, November 15, 2004.

125 Centre for Addiction and Mental Health. *Monitor 2002*. Cited in Ontario Tobacco Reduction Unit, "Indicators of OTS Progress," Toronto, 2004.

126 *Ontario Student Drug Use Survey, 2003*. Cited in Ontario Tobacco Reduction Unit, "Indicators of OTS Progress," Toronto, 2004.

127 Physicians for a Smoke-Free Canada. *Quitting Smoking. Findings from the Canadian Tobacco Use Monitoring Survey*. Ottawa, 2004.

128 R. Ferrence. "Learning from tobacco: bans on commercial availability are not unthinkable." *Addiction*, 2003, 93, 717-723.

129 National Cancer Institute. *Monograph 2: Smokeless Tobacco or Health: An International Perspective*. Smoking and Tobacco Control Monographs. 1992. Chapter 7, p. 318.

130 Lemieux, Pierre. "The Dangers of Tobacco Prohibition." *The Financial Post*, March 19, 2001, p. C-12.

131 Health Canada. *Quick Reference Guide to the Hazardous Products Act for Manufacturers, Importers, Distributors and Retailers*. www.hc-sc.gc.ca/hecs-sesc/cps/publications/hpa/intro.htm Accessed March 14, 2004.

132 Government of Canada. *Hazardous Products Act*, (R.S. 1985, c. H-3)

133 *Ibid.*, Part I of Schedule 1.

134 Health Canada. *Health Canada reminds Canadians not to use products containing kava*. http://www.hc-sc.gc.ca/english/protection/warnings/2003/2003_103.htm. Accessed March 14, 2004.

Chapter 4

135 More information available at: www.vancity.com.

136 More information at: www.mec.ca

137   More information at: www.goodwill.org.

138   Canadian Co-operative Association. *About Co-operatives*. 2004.

139   More information at: www.desjardins.com.

140   More information at: www.mec.ca.

141   Canadian Co-operative Association. *About Co-operatives*. 2004,

142   Canadian Co-operative Association. *Statistics*. 2004.

143   Mountain Equipment Co-op. *Annual Report*. 2003. pp.18-19. Overall Mondragon sales, including the financial group and the distribution group, were over 9 billion Euros.

144   Canadian Co-operative Association. *About Co-operatives*. 2004,

145   For example, British Columbia. *Cooperative Association Act*, section 8(2)(e)(v) [SBC 1999] C. 28. See also 7(1)(g)(iv) of the *Canada Cooperatives Act* (1998, c.1)

146   Government of Canada. *Canada Corporations Act*, Part II (S.C. 1970, c.C-32).

147   Generally, charitable status is available to organizations that serve religious purposes, alleviate poverty, carry out education, or engage in a handful of other, narrower areas that the courts have deemed charitable. Charities are not allowed to act outside of those purposes, or they are at risk of losing their charitable status.

148   Canada Revenue Agency. *Policy Statement. What is a Related Business?* Reference Number. CPS – 019. Ottawa.

149   Canada Revenue Agency. *Charities Summary Policy*. CSP - D15. Ottawa, September 3, 2003.

150   Hydro Quebec. *Annual Report 2003*.

151   Imperial Tobacco Canada. *Annual Information Form for the Year Ended December 31, 2003* at p.4 (market share) and 8 (total assets).

152   Canada Post. *Annual Report*. 2005.

153   Imperial Tobacco Canada. *Annual Information Form for the Year Ended December 31, 2003* at p.6 (1,400 employees).

154   Special Operating Agencies emerged in the late 1980s as a new government tool for service delivery (as distinct from policy advice). These agencies are given greater management flexibility and autonomy in order to allow them to achieve specified results. "Each SOA operates under a departmentally approved business plan. In addition, an accountability relationship within the department is defined by its framework document, which also lays out target commitments for service levels and financial performance." (source: http://www.tbs-sct.gc.ca/pubs_pol/opepubs/TB_B4/SOA_e.asp). The passport office, printing bureaus and information technology centres have been designated as special operating agencies.

155   N.T. Jazairi. *The Impact of Privatizing the Liquor Control Board of Ontario*. Department of Economics: York University, 1994 at p.5.

156 United Kingdom Department of Trade and Industry. *Community Interest Corporations*. London, 2004.

157 United Kingdom Department of Trade and Industry. *Community Interest Corporations Frequently Asked Questions*. London, 2004.

158 United Kingdom Department of Trade and Industry. *An Introduction to Community Interest Companies*. London, 2004.

159 United Kingdom Department of Trade and Industry. *Finance for CIC*. London, 2003.

160 United Kingdom Department of Trade and Industry. *An Introduction to Community Interest Companies*. London, 2004.

161 United Kingdom Department of Trade and Industry. *Finance for CIC*. March 2003. London, 2004.

162 United Kingdom Department of Trade and Industry. *Finance for CIC*. London, 2003.

163 United Kingdom Department of Trade and Industry. *Community Interest Corporations Frequently Asked Questions*. "3. Community Interest Test." London, 2004.

164 United Kingdom Department of Trade and Industry. *An Introduction to Community Interest Companies*. London, 2004.

165 United Kingdom Department of Trade and Industry. *Community Interest Corporations Frequently Asked Questions*. 5. Regulation.

166 Government of Canada. *Speech from the Throne*. Ottawa, 2004

167 Minister of industry. *Bill C-21. An Act Respecting Not-for-profit Corporations and Other Corporations Without Share Capital*. 2004.

168 UK Department of Trade and Industry. *Information Paper On Community Interest Companies: International Comparisons*. Undated, at p.4.

169 *Ibid.*, at p.6.

170 *Ibid.*

171 *Ibid.*, at p.11.

172 A. Breton, *A Conceptual Basis for an Industrial Strategy*, Ottawa: Economic Council of Canada, 1974.

173 New Democratic Party of Canada. *NDP Green Car Industrial Strategy Backgrounder*. Ottawa, 2004.

174 Imperial Tobacco. *Annual Report*, 2004.

175 World Trade Agreement. *General Agreement on Tariffs and Trade*, article XXI(b), Geneva: 1986; *General Agreement on Trade in Services*, article XIV bis (b), Marrakesh: 1994; *Agreement on Trade–Related Aspects of Intellectual Property*, article 73(b), Marrakesh: 1994.

176 Department of Foreign Affairs and International Trade. *Answers to Questions about Canada's Export Controls on Military Goods*. Ottawa, 1997.

177 Government of Canada. *A Discussion Paper on Canada's Contribution to Addressing Climate Change.* Ottawa: Government of Canada, 2002.

178 Natural Resources Canada. Office of Energy Efficiency, Natural Resources Canada. *Canadian Industry Program for Energy Conservation* (CIPEC).

179 For example, Ed Ricard, director of market strategy and development for Imperial Tobacco Canada, testified in the Quebec Superior Court in January 2002 that "target markets are always represented in terms of adult smokers."

180 Liquor Control Board of Ontario. *Annual Report.* 2002.

181 Nanuntsiaq News. "GN repatriates liquor." January 28, 2005. ("The possession of liquor will continue to be illegal in Nunavut's eight dry communities: Arviat, Coral Harbour, Gjoa Haven, Kimmirut, Pangnirtung, Kugaaruk, Sanikiluaq and Whale Cove.")

182 Convenience Store News. *Vendors Lose Tobacco-display privileges.* April 4, 2005.

183 Centre for Addiction and Mental Health. *Position Paper: Retail Alcohol Monopolies: Preserving the Public Interest.* Toronto. 1993.

184 *Ibid.*

185 *Ibid.*

186 *Ibid.*

187 *Ibid.*

188 R. Room. *Why Have a Retail Alcohol Monopoly.* Paper presented at an International Seminar on Alcohol Retail Monopolies, Harrisburg, Pennsylvania, August 19-21, 2001.

189 G.A. Austin. *Perspectives on the History of Psychoactive Substance Use.* National Institute for Drug Addiction Research Issues 24, DHEW Publication No. (ADM) 79-810. Washington: USGPO, 1978 11, 14. Quoted in Room, Robin "The Evolution of Alcohol Monopolies and their Relevance for Public Health." *Contemporary Drug Problems.* 20: 169-187, 1993.

190 Council for a Smoke-Free PEI. *Retail Sale of Tobacco Products on PEI, A Brief Submitted to the Standing Committee on Social Development.* February, 2004

191 Alberta Gaming Research Institute. *Legalized gambling in Canada.* 2002.

192 P.J. Garfield et al. *Public Utility Economics.* Englewood Cliffs, New Jersey: Prentice-Hall Inc., 1964. 15-24.

193 C. Armstrong and H.V. Nelles, *Monopoly's Moment: The Organization and Regulation of Canadian Utilities: 1830-1930.* Toronto: University of Toronto Press, 1988. 325-327.

194 Government of Canada. *Canada Health Act.*

195 Heritage Canada Web-site. http://www.canadianheritage.gc.ca/index_e.cfm.

196 Government of Canada. *Broadcasting Act*, 1991, s. 3(1)(d)(i).

197 Department of Canadian Heritage. *Guide to Canadian Heritage Financial Support Programs Spring 2004 Creating Canada Together*. Ottawa, 2004.

198 Department of Canadian Heritage. *New International Instrument on Cultural Diversity (NIICD)*, 2005.

Chapter 5

199 See, for example, the factums of provincial and federal governments found in *Government of Saskatchewan and Rothmans, Benson & Hedges Inc., Compilation of Factums, Supreme Court of Canada file NO. 29973*.

200 LaForest, J, in *RJR-MacDonald Inc. v. Canada* (Attorney General) [1995] 3 S.C.R. 199 at para.43. Although LaForest J. dissented on the final disposition of the case on Charter grounds, the majority adopted his reasons on the criminal law powers of Parliament (at para. 181). Available at http://www.lexum. umontreal.ca/csc-scc/en/pub /1995/vol3/html/ 1995scr3_0199.html. This judgment also points out the clear authority to create exemptions (paras.52-56), such as the exemption for the public interest tobacco manufacturer.

201 *Rothmans, Benson & Hedges Inc. v. Saskatchewan* (2005) S.C.C. 13. Available at http://www.lexum.umontreal.ca/csc-scc/en/rec/html /2005scc013. wpd.html.

202 *Irwin toy ltd. v. Quebec* (Attorney general), [1989] 1 S.C.R. 927.

203 *Canadian Egg Marketing Agency v. Richardson*, [1998] 3 S.C.R. 157 at para. 104-105.

204 A complete list of trade agreements to which Canada is signatory can be found at http://www.dfait-maeci.gc.ca/tna-nac/.

205 World Trade Organization. *General Agreement on Tariffs and Trade*, Article XI.

206 World Trade Organization. *General Agreement on Tariffs and Trade*, Article III, North American Free Trade Agreement, Article 301.

207 World Trade Organization. *Thailand – Restrictions on Importation of and Internal taxes on cigarettes. Report of the Panel adopted on 7 November 1990* (DS10/R - 37S/200), at paragraph 79.

208 *North American Free Trade Agreement*. Chapter 15.

209 Health Canada makes public the sales data reported to it by tobacco corporations in compliance with regulations under the *Tobacco Act*, 1997.

210 The record of decisions in this case is available on the World Trade Organization web-site (www.wto.org).

211 World Trade Organization. *Ministerial Declaration*. 20 November 2001.

212 The text of the *Framework Convention on Tobacco Control* can be found at www.fctc.org.

213 United Nations High Commission for Refugees - Committee on Economic, Social and Cultural Rights. *The Right to the Highest Attainable Standards of Health*: 04/07/2000.E/C.12/2000/.4, CESR General comment 14, para 51.

214 Competition Bureau. *Annual Report 1999/2000* - Reviewing Mergers.

215 Canadian Press. *Cigarette Makers Rothmans, BAT Announce Merger,* Monday Jan 11, 1999.

216 B. Marotte. "Global Cigarette Giant British American Tobacco's stake in Toronto-based Rothmans Inc. is Going for $314 million, Less Than Half its Value a Year Ago." *CanWest News,* Feb 4, 2000.]

217 Canadian Press. "Imasco Shares Up in Smoke; Tobacco Giant Buyout Worth $10.7 billion" *The Windsor Star.* Windsor, Ont.: Jan 29, 2000.

218 Imperial Tobacco. *Annual Report.* 2004.

219 Royal Canadian Mounted Police. *RCMP Lays Criminal Charges Against Canadian Tobacco Company.* Toronto, 2003.

220 M.J. Kaiserman. "The Cost of Smoking in Canada, 1991." *Chronic diseases in Canada,* Volume 18, No.1 -1997.

221 Canadian Cancer Society. *Canadian Cancer Statistics.* 2004, p. 55.

222 Total figures on all government expenditures have not been made public: federal expenditures are under $80 million per year, and combined provincial expenditures are estimated as being no greater. (Personal correspondence, Health Canada).

Chapter 6

223 *RJR-MacDonald Inc. v. Canada* (Attorney General) [1995] 3 S.C.R. 199 at para.36.

224 Health and Welfare Canada. *National Strategy To Reduce Tobacco Use, 1985.*

225 Health Canada, *New Directions for Tobacco Control in Canada. A National Strategy, 1999.*

226 Health Canada. *The Federal Tobacco Control Strategy.* 2002.

227 Health Canada. *Canadian Tobacco Use Monitoring Survey.* 2004 (wave 1).

228 Imperial Tobacco. *Annual Reports,* 2000-2004.

229 Private communication, March 2005.

230 Physicians for a Smoke-Free Canada. *Background on Protection from Second-Hand Smoke in Canada,* 2005.

231 Determined by conducting key word searches for "ending," "prohibition," "banning" at www.tobaccocontrol.com on April 4, 2005.

232 Health Canada. *Federal Tobacco Control Strategy.* Ottawa, 2001.

233 Examples include D. Sweanor. "Regulatory imbalance between medicinal and non-medicinal nicotine." *Addiction,* Supplement 1, 2000.

234 J. Liberman. "Where to for tobacco regulation: time for new approaches?" *Drug and Alcohol Review,* Vol. 22, Issue 4, 461-469.

235 R. Borland et al. A strategy for controlling the marketing of tobacco products: a regulated market model. *Tobacco Control*: 2003: 12, 374-382.

236 Environics. *Focus Canada 2004-3.* A survey of 2047 respondents.

237 Susan Bondy et al. "Past trends in tobacco use and some thoughts on future trends," in Roberta Ferrence et al. *Nicotine and Public Health*, American Public Health Association, 2000.

238 J. Prochaska & C. DiClemente. "Stages and processes of self-change in smoking: Toward an integrative model of change." *Journal of Consulting and Clinical Psychology*, 51, 390-395.

239 NHS Stop Smoking Service. www.dh.gov.uk.

240 H. Selin. *The Mythical Canadian Cigar Craze*. Non-smokers Rights Association. March 1998.

241 Health Canada/Attorney General of Canada. *Comparison between the Tobacco Products Control (TPCA) and Tobacco Sales to Young Persons Acts (TSYPA) and the Tobacco Act*. Written pleadings filed by the Attorney General of Canada with the Quebec Superior Court, 2002.

242 Attorney General of Canada. *Tobacco Act Challenge*. Written pleadings filed by the Attorney General of Canada with the Quebec Superior Court, 2002.

243 Washington National Weekly Edition. December 9-15, 1996, p. 8 quoted in D. Moyer. *Tobacco Reference Guide*. www.tobaccoprogram.org. Accessed March 2004.

244 Personal correspondence.

245 Altria. Press Release: *Illinois Trial Judge Says Philip Morris USA Must Post Higher Bond In Price Case; Company Will Await Supreme Court Action*. August 15, 2003.

246 J. Caher. "N.Y. Bill Would Cap Tobacco Suit Appeal Bonds." *New York Law Journal*, July 26, 2004.

247 *In the matter of the Companies' Creditors Arrangement Act, RSC 1985, c. C-36, as amended and in the Matter of JTI-Macdonald Corp*, Notice of Application dated August 24, 2004.

248 Extrapolating from reports by Health Canada's Canadian Tobacco Use Monitoring Survey that there are 400,000 Canadians aged 15–19 who smoke.